Marlon Brando

Marlon Brando

Anatomy of an Actor

CAHIERS DU CINEMA

Marlon Brando

Florence Colombani

Introduction 7

1 Stanley Kowalski 12
A Streetcar Named Desire (1951)
Elia Kazan

2 Mark Antony 28
Julius Caesar (1953)
Joseph L. Mankiewicz

3 Terry Malloy 44
On the Waterfront (1954)
Elia Kazan

4 Napoleon Bonaparte 60
Désirée (1954)
Henry Koster

5 Rio 76
One-Eyed Jacks (1961)
Marlon Brando

6 Fletcher Christian 92
Mutiny on the Bounty (1962)
Lewis Milestone

7 Major Weldon Penderton 108
Reflections in a Golden Eye (1967)
John Huston

8 Don Vito Corleone 124
The Godfather (1972)
Francis Ford Coppola

9 Paul 140
Last Tango in Paris (1972)
Bernardo Bertolucci

10 Colonel Walter E. Kurtz 156
Apocalypse Now (1979)
Francis Ford Coppola

Conclusion 173
Chronology 177
Filmography 181
Bibliography 186
Notes 187
Index 190

Introduction

"Here was a Caesar! When comes such another?"
—William Shakespeare, *Julius Caesar* (act III, scene 2)

In the fall of 1957, the writer Truman Capote visited the set of *Sayonara* in the ancient imperial city of Kyoto. His goal? To get up close to the reigning prince of the excessively American aristocracy of film stars, to warm himself for a moment in the rays of the most radiant of stars, to penetrate the mystery of Marlon Brando. Gifted with exceptional sensitivity, the novelist seems to have fulfilled his mission. He spent hours in private with the actor, pouring sake when his glass was empty and drawing out some real secrets. Brando would hold it against him, incidentally, as he would with anyone—various journalists and directors—who, by ruse or by force, succeeded in getting him to divulge something about himself. "Sensitive people are so vulnerable," explained Brando to Capote in his hotel room while awaiting his usual gargantuan feast. "They're so easily brutalized and hurt just because they *are* sensitive. The more sensitive you are, the more certain you are to be brutalized, develop scabs."[1] Sensitive is indeed what Brando had to be to fill his characters with such intensity and to color them with such subtle nuances. Yet what's especially striking when reading his autobiography, *Songs My Mother Taught Me*,[2] or one of his interviews from that time, is how many scabs there were, and how thick. King of kings during a period no doubt less cruel toward its celebrities than our own, Marlon Brando succeeded, for over half a century—until the tragedy his family experienced in the 1990s—in protecting himself from too much media exposure. As a young man, he met innumerable journalists, gave interviews freely, and yet, all in all, revealed little. When he recalls his relationship with his father in Truman Capote's portrait of him, it comes as a shock. Years later, in 1991, Lawrence Grobel published a book of interviews that promised treasures, an up-close portrait of the real Brando, captured during the intimate moments he spent with his family on his Tahitian atoll. Alas, despite revealing bits, the interview remained vague as soon as it touched on the actor's craft or even on cinema in general. As for Brando's memoirs, written during a period of profound emotional and financial distress, they give the impression that the mystery surrounding the star only thickens once the book is closed. This brings to mind Joshua Logan, the director of *Sayonara* (1957), who confided to Capote, "Marlon's the most exciting person I've met since Garbo. A genius. But I don't know what he's like. I don't know anything about him."

The Early Years

Throughout his childhood, Marlon Brando Junior was called Bud. He was Bud to his school friends in Omaha, Nebraska, where he was born in 1924, Bud to his parents—Marlon Senior and Dodie—and to his sisters—Jocelyn, his little mama, and Frances, his accomplice in mischievous childhood wrongdoing. Educated at Shattuck Military Academy, Marlon Senior worked as an engineer for Western Limestone, while his wife, a real rising star on the local scene, successfully took on leading roles at the city's central theater, even sharing the billing with a young Henry Fonda. Slowly but surely, the Brando couple broke down due to alcohol and domestic disputes. The children were left on their own when Dodie took off for Kansas City with one of her short-term lovers or when Marlon Senior spent the night frequenting speakeasies. In 1930, the Brandos left Omaha for Chicago, where a new and better-paid job awaited the head of the family. Thus ended, as quickly as it had begun, Dodie's budding career. A friend from that time told Peter Manso: "She also used to quip, 'I'm the greatest actress *not* on the American stage'. She thought she was better than Katharine Cornell, and the only time I asked, 'Then why in hell are you letting it go?' all she said was, 'Three kids.'"[3] Fueled by so much frustration and unhappiness, the demon drink tightened its grip on the Brando couple. The three children lived in fear of their parents' fights, terrifying flashes of violence that Marlon would rediscover, as though they'd eluded his aching memory, decades later during a performance of *Who's Afraid of Virgina Woolf?*

With his already striking good looks and a violent temperament, the young Bud did not go unnoticed. Even though the schoolteacher called his parents in, hoping to inform them of their son's serious lack of discipline, no one ever showed up to the meeting. When he skipped school, the kid wandered around a Prohibition-era Chicago, a disreputable town of gangsters and drunkards that he came to know like the back of his hand. Together with his buddies, he hot-wired cars in parking lots and broke into houses in upscale neighborhoods for the sheer thrill of the forbidden. His friendships offered him fleeting substitute families. Byron Veiris, a schoolmate, realized that if Bud visited him with such enthusiasm, it was particularly to see his mother. "He almost seemed to revere her. Some of it was envying our family, longing for something like it. Even when he stuck around after dark, there were never phone calls from the Brando household looking for him."[4] When he turned twelve, his parents decided to make a new start. They chose a small town with a highly symbolic name, Libertyville, where they rented an isolated farm and its many animals—dogs, hens, goats, and even a cow that Bud had to milk morning and night. In junior high, not only did people notice his insolence, his physical agility, and his symmetrical features, but also his sudden mood swings and his unpredictable temperament: his classmates, like his costars later on, complained about never knowing what to expect. Even then there were the tasteless jokes, preferably as humiliating for him as for others, which greatly resembled the deplorable tricks he'd later play on movie sets. And finally he established his odd way of mumbling that exasperated his teachers, as it later would theater critics.

At school, Bud seemed to be a dunce, but at home, he devoured Fitzgerald, Shakespeare, and all the classics in his mother's library. Whether it was the result of this secret passion for books or of his boundless admiration for the lovely Dodie, he signed up for a drama class. Did this lost child, neglected by his mother and mistreated by his father, understand at once that he had found a way out of his unhappiness? Did he feel a marvelous sense of relief, the certainty that all would be well? We'd like to believe this, and yet, here again, Bud hardly won people over: too much of a loner, rude to his friends, always taking advantage, insolent—what teacher would want him? It's hard not to make the connection between his behavior and the family chaos that rarely let up. Dodie made several unsuccessful suicide attempts. Marlon Senior openly scorned his strapping son who dreamed of becoming an actor, a career for pansies. Bud picked a fight anywhere he could find it, to the point of getting kicked out of high school. There he was, at seventeen, forced to follow in his father's footsteps, straight to Shattuck Military Academy.

The Teachings of Stella Adler

Marlon Senior soon had to face the facts: as creative and ingenious as Bud was when it came to annoying others, he had no talent for academics. Far from discovering in himself any kind of military vocation, the young Brando understood—thanks to the Shattuck theater club—that his place was on stage, a strategic location his mother had unfortunately and reluctantly left behind. The need to make up for their mother's tragedy was also felt by his older sisters, who struck out on their own and began careers as actresses. During school vacation, while Dodie ran off to drink, the two Marlons stayed alone, locked in a fierce debate with no resolution. The military institution put an end to this long duel one day by expelling Marlon following a scandal that remains rather mysterious. Thus Brando Senior gave up and sent his son to New York, where he shared an apartment with his sister Frances and enrolled in the Dramatic Workshop, founded by the German director Erwin Piscator. The classes were not only practical—though many of them did focus on makeup, diction, dance, and acrobatics. Theory also had its place: they studied Stanislavski, Freud, and the great actors of the European tradition. Very soon, Stella Adler, one of the professors, noticed Marlon and made him her protégé. He became a part of her family, accompanied her to museums and concerts, and finally benefited from a true education.

Stella Adler was an attractive figure: the daughter of a famous Yiddish actor, a student of Stanslavski in Paris, and a marvelous professor— "a spirited and flamboyant teacher," writes Kazan in his memoirs, "who emphasizes characterization and role interpretation rather than emotional recall."[5] The Stanislavski Method, as taught at the Actors Studio, is well-known for using technical exercises to encourage actors to draw out at any moment of a scene authentic emotions from their personal memories. This recourse to sensory and emotional memory guarantees the sincerity of the interpretation: truly overcome— because he has called up, for example, the memory of grieving—the actor has every chance of being excellent. Lee Strasberg, long-time director of the Actors Studio, was the authority among American adepts of this famous Method. Brando is most often seen as its best ambassador, the very incarnation of the Method's success. It's true that he paved the way for a whole new generation of actors, such as James Dean or Paul Newman, who attentively followed the Actors Studio's training and later did it justice. But note that the Actors Studio was founded in 1947, the year Brando starred in the Broadway production of *A Streetcar Named Desire*. Brando's success is therefore not attributable to it. It was really, in his case, the teaching of Stella Adler that was decisive and not his occasional visits, intended above all to measure his popularity among students, to Lee Strasberg's school. The nuance

is important, for Strasberg and Adler, archenemies, had distinct approaches to the actor's craft. "Brando said he found unbearable Strasberg's focus on the actor's own underlying personality,"[6] notes Peter Bogdanovich. Adler's idea was the opposite — actors have to be detached from themselves, for "Drama depends on doing, not feeling; feeling is a by-product of doing." Which is to say that acting comes down to movement more than thought. She encouraged "subtle, creative, onstage choices," without depriving actors of the "imagination to locate the fullest range" of the character's motivations "rather than depending solely on their personal past and emotional memory."[7] The dig at Strasberg is clear. Upon his death, Adler came into class and proclaimed — after a ritual minute of silence — that it would take a hundred years to repair the damage that man did to the theater. In other words, while she recognized the value of an intimate memory put to the service of a character, Stella Adler placed much more trust in technique for constructing an interpretation. Thus her training also included classes in makeup, voice, mime, acrobatics, and the history of theater. Traces of these classes, which Brando was enthused about, can be found in his work. If he accepted *The Teahouse of the August Moon* (1956), it was primarily for the pleasure of making himself up like the Japanese.

In *The Godfather* (1972), he invented the bulldog head of Don Corleone himself, by stuffing tissues in his cheeks. With Chaplin (*A Countess from Hong Kong*, 1967), as in his sole musical comedy (*Guys and Dolls*, 1955), he revealed his agility as a dancer.

After Strasberg's death, in his preface to the first edition of *The Technique of Acting*, the book Stella Adler published in 1988, Brando also attacked the famous "Method" inspired by Stanislavski and popularized by Strasberg. Stella, he explains, "never lent herself to vulgar exploitations, as some other well-known so-called 'methods' of acting have done. As a result, her contributions to the theatrical culture have remained largely unknown, unrecognized, and unappreciated."[8] Let's forget the old family quarrels. "Marlon, well trained by Stella Adler, had excellent technique," recalls Elia Kazan, who distinguishes him in this regard from James Dean. "He was proficient in every aspect of acting, including characterization and makeup. He was also a great mimic."[9] All things conveniently forgotten by the legend that expects a genius to be a "natural." And yet, when Marlon Brando electrified the crowds in *A Streetcar Named Desire* (1951), he didn't settle for being Stanley Kowalski on stage: he played his role with an already accomplished art. And achieved a realistic effect so convincing that everyone was taken in by it.

This book was inspired by a question: Is it possible to put our finger on what makes Marlon Brando such a great actor? To track down his genius, understand its essence? Perhaps, but it requires precision. So we've chosen ten films starring Brando and decided to study them from their conception to their release. We will thus follow the genesis and the creation of a few obvious masterpieces (*Streetcar*, *On the Waterfront*, *The Godfather*, *Apocalypse Now*) and a shocking film that reveals more of him than all the others combined (*Last Tango in Paris*, 1972), a piercing literary adaptation (*Reflections in a Golden Eye*, 1967), and the love story of a great historical figure (*Désirée*, 1954). Above all, we'll get into the details of each performance. Who is the character and how does Brando portray him? How does he go about playing Napoleon or Colonel Kurtz? Gestures, voice inflections, looks: these are the clues that will allow us to understand his Stanley Kowalski and his Vito Corleone. Is Brando the same in the loving eyes of his spiritual father, Elia Kazan, or when he is himself directing (*One-Eyed Jacks*, 1961)? How does he do with Shakespeare's verse (*Julius Caesar*, 1953) and with Fletcher Christian's stubborn silences (*Mutiny on the Bounty*, 1962)? Answering these questions assumes first and foremost some self-reliant detective work. In the numerous interviews he gave over the course of his life, the actor spewed scornful comments on his art and refused to reveal the slightest secret, except for a few snatches from his painful childhood.

Admittedly, Brando shot his share of duds, but limiting ourselves to only ten roles of course leaves us with a few regrets: the passionate revolutionary in *Viva Zapata!* (1952), the magnificent drifter in *The Fugitive Kind* (1959), or the decadent gardener in *The Nightcomers* (1971). Through the ten roles we'll stop to consider here, a repertoire of gestures takes shape, as does a surprisingly consistent philosophy of the craft of acting. A bit of the history of twentieth century art is also told, from the thunderclap of his Kowalski in *Streetcar* on Broadway, with his dazzling virility, to the overwhelming rawness of *Last Tango in Paris* twenty-five years later and the mumbling he popularized as *The Godfather*, from Elia Kazan to Francis Ford Coppola. To study Marlon Brando the actor is to retrace the evolution of cinema over half a century, following a sometimes winding path that crosses that of major contemporary authors (Tennessee Williams, Carson McCullers) and mythic actors (Elizabeth Taylor, Al Pacino), and that calls into question the present time (the mafia of New York's dockworkers, the Vietnam War) while re-creating the past.

Brando the actor works with a single medium: Brando the man. Beyond the blinding beauty of his early years, the shaven head and heavyset body of *Apocalypse Now*, we can make out, faintly, the course of a life that didn't fulfill its promise, an existence shattered from the beginning, and that continued on with sound and fury. From the start there were fits of bulimia and marked emotional distress. And then the tragedy occurred: Christian Brando killed Dag Drollet, the boyfriend of his half sister Cheyenne. The young woman committed suicide shortly thereafter. Marlon dreamed of being a Tahitian patriarch and ended his life in hallucinatory solitude, a sad emperor reigning over a field of ruins. "For there was a mixture of self-pity and self-destructiveness in Mr. Brando that could not endure the toxic diet of straight American success," wrote David Thomson by way of eulogy in 2004.[10] It's this extremely sensitive personality, with its exacerbated vulnerability, that moves us so deeply the more it is poorly disguised beneath the shell of a role or the goodwill of a director. All that Brando sought to hide his whole life long is exposed there, on the screen, for all the world to see. And if the effect produced is captivating to this extent, and at times overwhelming, it's because we're not dealing with an involuntary or rash exposure but rather with a conscious process, the result of a well-honed technique—in short, an authentic artistic approach. So in these pages we will consider Marlon Brando the actor and Marlon Brando the auteur: an artist who left us an inconsistent body of work, perhaps, but one that's just as passionate and, above all, unparalleled.

1

Stanley Kowalski

A Streetcar Named Desire (1951)
Elia Kazan

"I guess I'm gonna strike you as being the unrefined type, huh?"
— Stanley Kowalski

Stanley Kowalski! Only slightly less famous than that of Marlon Brando, the name Kowalski instantly evokes the same image. A twenty-five-year-old hunk with tousled hair and full lips wearing a skin-tight T-shirt. He leans against a wall, his arms crossed and his brow furrowed. "No matter […] what cast," wrote Elia Kazan in his memoirs, each new production of *A Streetcar Named Desire* "was always hailed, often as 'better than the original production.' What could I say to that? Bravo, Tennessee!"[11] Sorry to contradict Kazan, a close friend of Tennessee Williams and the brilliant director of the Broadway debut of *Streetcar* as well as of its Hollywood adaptation, but where did he get the idea that casting the role of Stanley Kowalski wasn't a problem? Or that each new production is deemed to have surpassed the original? Just open a paper after a new production premieres and you'll notice the complete opposite. Take *Variety*. When *Streetcar* was staged in New York by Liv Ullmann in 2009 — sixty-two years after it was written — with Cate Blanchett in the role of Blanche, the critic David Rooney complimented Joel Edgerton on "a performance indebted to the defining mold of Marlon Brando."[12] Another example: more than twenty years after *Streetcar* was created, while having one of her students work on a scene, Stella Adler suddenly shouted, "Stop it! Marlon isn't like that!"[13] Marlon instead of Stanley. The truth is that in the history of theater there's no actor and role have come together quite like Marlon Brando and Stanley Kowalski.

From Broadway to Hollywood

A factory worker from New Orleans, Stanley Kowalski is a guy who likes to play poker, drink beer, lay his young wife, Stella, and does not want to answer to anybody. Nor does he appreciate the arrival of his sister-in-law, Blanche, a delicate and extremely sensitive creature, who shows up for an indeterminate length of time with a huge suitcase and bad news: debts have led to the loss of the family estate, Belle Reve. Thus begins a merciless struggle between Blanche and Stanley

that ends with the total victory of the gloating he-man and the committal of the wounded woman. Since its premiere on December 3, 1947, the play has been regarded as a modern classic. The *New York Herald Tribune* critic Howard Barnes introduced Tennessee Williams as "the Eugene O'Neill of the present period."[14] Wolcott Gibbs of the *New Yorker* raved about this "brilliant, implacable play about the disintegration of a woman, or, if you like, of a society."[15] It won the Pulitzer Prize as well as the New York Drama Critics' Circle Award. And that's the least you can say about this "masterful work, written out of Tennessee's most personal experience," a masterpiece so full of lyricism and despair that there is "no way to spoil."[16] Struck by its perfection, the contemporary reader of *A Streetcar Named Desire* is amazed by the extreme precision of the stage directions, the almost topographical description of the sole set — Stanley and Stella's dreary apartment — and the mention of particular movements or facial expressions that the author expects from the actors. Did Tennessee Williams incorporate his own direction into the text? Did he forget about the liberty that is indispensable to the artists who bring a theatrical work to life? On the contrary, he simply included in the final script the directorial choices made by Elia Kazan and his actors: Jessica Tandy (Blanche), Kim Hunter (Stella), Karl Malden (Mitch)… and Marlon Brando, the one and only Stanley Kowalski. If we're left with the impression of knowing this production, it's because the same actors (except for Jessica Tandy, replaced by Vivien Leigh) reprised their roles in the film version produced a few years after the Broadway production by Elia Kazan, who was anxious to record the work they'd accomplished and to pay homage to a script he deeply loved.

Of course, the best and the brightest have grappled with this fundamental work of Americana, this splendid tragedy of the South's decline. In Italy, Luchino Visconti staged *Streetcar*, with no less than Vittorio Gassman (Stanley) and Marcello Mastroianni (Mitch). In England, Sir Laurence Olivier was contracted, and he gave the role of Blanche to his wife, Vivien Leigh. In France, Raymond Rouleau directed Arletty to create a portrait of Blanche that was predictably Parisian. Would Kazan see Alec Baldwin take on

Marlon Brando on the set of Elia Kazan's *A Streetcar Named Desire* (1951).

Marlon Brando and director Elia Kazan.

Opposite: Marlon Brando on the set of the film.

Following pages: Marlon Brando, Ruby Bond, Karl Malden and Kim Hunter.

the role of Stanley on Broadway a full decade before the director's death?[17] Ultimately, regardless of the performers' prestige or the directors' fame, no Stanley Kowalski has managed to banish the ghost of Marlon Brando. The actor himself would confide to Truman Capote: "Tennessee has made a fixed association between me and Kowalski. I mean, we're friends and he knows that as a person I am just the opposite of Kowalski, who was everything I'm against — totally insensitive, crude, cruel. But still Tennessee's image of me is confused with the fact that I played that part. So I don't know if he could write for me in a different color range."[18]

A Tailor-Made Role?

Must we, like Kazan, the genius behind this wonderful encounter, have the strong feeling that Brando and Kowalski are twins? Was Stanley only half a challenge for Brando, insofar as the character resembled him like a brother?[19] Tennessee Williams was blown away when he saw the unknown actor that Kazan had sent him — fresh from his appearance in *Truckline Cafe*[20] — because he looked so much like the Kowalski of Williams's imagination. He forgot that Brando was only twenty-four while his Stanley was thirty. However, according to Truman Capote, who met him at the time, Brando in no way evoked "Williams' unpoetic Kowalski."[21]

The actress playing Stella, Kim Hunter, assured that "Stanley is very apart from Marlon."[22] In his memoirs, the playwright recounts how he didn't care either way; all that mattered on that blessed day was that he found himself standing before "just about the best-looking young man [he'd] ever seen."[23] That sounds like Stella: "Isn't he wonderful looking?" she asks her sister as she points him out to her for the first time in the bowling alley. Stanley Kowalski — a Pole, not a Polack, as he stresses in a famous scene — is, the stage directions specify, "of medium height, about five feet eight or nine, and strongly, compactly built. Animal joy in his being is implicit in all his movements and attitudes. [He has] the power and pride of a richly feathered male bird" who reigns over the henhouse. Moreover, he "sizes women up at a glance, with sexual classifications, crude images flashing into his mind and determining the way he smiles at them."[24] And yet Williams realized in an instant that Brando's profound nature corresponded deeply with his character. He had the same vitality, the prodigious sexual appetite, the liking for manipulating others, sometimes teasingly, sometimes cruelly. The young actor subjected Jessica Tandy — his costar — to genuine psychological abuse, not so far removed from the perilous game of cat and mouse that Stanley inflicts on Blanche to the point of causing her to snap. "In the birthday scene," recounts Peter

Manso, Brando's biographer, "she thought he was deliberately rattling the dishes—not as a dramatic touch, but to disturb her whenever she came to her key lines. [...] Marlon planted a story with publicist Eddie Jaffe that Tandy had received death threats from one of her more ardent admirers. Soon the story appeared in the *Daily News*. [...] In the middle of one of her more emotional speeches, Tandy noticed giggling in the audience. Looking back at Brando, she observed him, stone-faced, shoving a cigarette up his nostril."[25] And there's no need to dwell on the scatological jokes and unexpected groans that interrupted his costars, or the obscenities murmured during the final scene to break Karl Malden's and Jessica Tandy's concentration.

A Confrontation Between Actors

Was the young Brando rude? Perhaps. But let's not forget that Blanche summed up his character in these words: "Thousands of years have passed him right by and there he is—Stanley Kowalski—survivor of the Stone Age! Bearing the raw meat home from the kill in the jungle!" In reality, the clash, on stage and in the wings, between Jessica Tandy and Marlon Brando imitated the one that structures the entire play. On one hand, there is the vulgarity, violence, and bestiality of Stanley. On the other hand, the taste for the marvelous and the fanciful, the refinement and elegance of

Blanche. Miss DuBois's struggle against her brother-in-law becomes, in the most lyrical moments of the play, that of poetry against prose, of fiction against reality. The story of an enchanting moth crushed in the tight fist of a thick brute. We can imagine, then, Kazan's dismay when he realized that Brando rallied all sides to the point where the audience wanted to see him crush Blanche. "When he derided Blanche, they responded with approving laughter. Was the play becoming the Marlon Brando Show?"[26] For her part, Jessica Tandy suffered greatly. "Night after night I had to fight that audience. I had to try to make them be with me, to sit and listen and understand."[27] Distraught, the actress—who had more than twenty-five years of professional experience—sought help from a therapist. When he asked her what was bothering her, her answer shot back resounded with defeat. Meanwhile, Kazan confided his worries to Tennessee Williams. The playwright reassured him as well as he could: "Blanche is not an angel without a flaw [...] and Stanley's not evil. I know you're used to clearly stated themes, but this play should not be loaded one way or the other. Don't try to simplify things."[28] The prevailing panic left Brando unmoved. The audience adored him, the critics praised him to the skies, and the author couldn't get enough of the way he cleared Blanche's birthday table—with a great clash of broken dishes. "It was kind

of a release for Tennessee; perhaps they were his mother's plates," Kazan mused.[29] But Brando, despite his hotheaded boyishness, had a profound respect for the play. "Some things you can ad-lib, some things you have to commit to memory, like Shakespeare, Tennessee Williams, where the language has value. You can't ad-lib Tennessee Williams," he would say years later, whereas from then on no other script would seem to him to be worthy of memorization.[30]

It's obvious in the film that Brando's all-consuming magnetism makes the play and its vision of human relationships more complex. As poetic as she may be, Blanche is not just a victim crushed by a violent and hostile man. From the first act she oscillates between reason and madness. Her breakdown—far from being explained solely by the pressure of Stanley—is also fated. "We've had this date with each other from the beginning!" Stanley tells her. And he's right: it's Blanche's rendezvous with herself. Echoing this idea, Tennessee Williams admitted that "She was a demonic creature, the size of her feeling was too great for her to contain without the escape of madness."[31] Played by an authentically seductive Brando, Stanley isn't just some demon who has sworn to do away with the heroine, a vile, despicable being that the audience rejects, but rather the trigger of Blanche Dubois's inevitable downfall. Bringing the play to the screen four years after it was first performed on stage, Kazan accentuated this dimension and thereby gave the play new depth. The choice of Vivien Leigh was key: the legendary star of *Gone with the Wind* (1939) was crucial in this sense. For Blanche is a kind of faded Scarlett O'Hara, a queen of flirtation who once ruled over a plantation, Belle Reve, not so far from Margaret Mitchell's Tara. When, wearing a tiara and alone before her mirror, she talks to herself and imagines regaling a crowd of suitors with her charming anecdotes, could it be that the tragic ghost of the resplendent heroine of Victor Fleming's film has appeared before our eyes? In the film, Blanche is infinitely poignant because she is enriched by our memory as filmgoers: the sight of this ruined Scarlett, abandoned and alone, is inevitably painful for those who recall her days of glory.

When she arrived in the United States to shoot the film, Vivien Leigh was utterly confused about her identity, to the point that she confessed, "I had nine months in the theatre of Blanche Dubois.[32] Now she's in command of me in Hollywood."[33] Moreover, during one of the fits of delirium that would punctuate her final years, all of a sudden a nurse who thought it would comfort her shouted, "I know who you are. You're Scarlett O'Hara, aren't you?" The actress snapped back at her, "I'm not Scarlett O'Hara. I'm Blanche DuBois."[34] Her obvious psychological fragility impacted Brando's attitude during the shooting. Though, it goes without saying, his acting method

left Miss Leigh perplexed. "You never know what he's going to do next, where he's going to be or what he's going to say," she complained, in a strikingly concise way, for herself and all of Brando's future costars.[35] His capacity to change things in each take has become legendary. His sudden sighs or murmurs interrupted the lines of other actors; his movements surprised them and drove the cameraman crazy. But what was surprising was that during the filming of *Streetcar*, there was no longer any trace of the maliciousness he expressed toward Jessica Tandy. To the contrary, with the beautiful Vivien Leigh, Brando played the ladies' man, a bit crass of course, but always civil, pleasantly teasing her about the love affair the tabloids always supposed they were having. And he got it right, judging by a production shot in which Vivien gazes upon his classically perfect profile most admiringly.

The result is that between the Blanche and Stanley of the film there's a subtle seductive connection that considerably increases the dramatic intensity. This is clear in Stanley's second appearance on screen—after the bowling scene where Blanche and Stella observe him from afar—in the kitchen of his dingy apartment. Suddenly he enters, facing a nervous yet smiling Blanche: "You must be Stanley. I'm Blanche." It's the start of a veritable choreography backed up wonderfully by Kazan's camerawork and the jazzy music of Alex North. Stanley unbuttons his jacket as he walks toward the camera, goes to the kitchen, where he leans back for a moment against the sink, and pours himself a drink. "Ordinarily, the camera would go to Vivien," Karl Malden recalled, "but it's following him scratching his back. See, he knows where to scratch."[36] Then, with arrogant ease, Stanley changes his T-shirt—"Be comfortable, that's my motto"—approaches Blanche and suddenly comes to a halt in front of her. He hasn't stopped moving since he entered the apartment, and so the camera has followed his every step. His abrupt immobility at once takes on a menacing quality. Stanley looks at Blanche, with a roving look that seems to take in her face and body at once. Piercing caterwauls startle her suddenly. Surprised, she lays her hand on Stanley's biceps. Still unblinking, he looks at his sister-in-law's hand on his arm, then raises his eyes—"Oh, those cats!"—and lets out a caterwaul that's truer than life. In his eyes, a wild joy, a wickedness that's irresistible and cruel.

The effect of this scene—the first confrontation between the two characters—is twofold. On the one hand, it suggests that the mutual and obvious attraction between Blanche and Stanley during this brief physical contact is dangerous. It leads to Stanley's unexpected wildcat wail, a clear symbol of his profound wildness. On the other hand, it establishes Stanley's bestiality as a fundamental element of his character. And it's no coincidence the scene takes place in the kitchen. The number of scenes throughout the film where Stanley eats or drinks is surprising. The first time we see him talking with Stella, he's fixated on what he's eating and barely raises his eyes to look at his wife. After that he always has chewing gum in his mouth, and in the biggest clashes of the film—Blanche's birthday party, the night he spends one-on-one with her because Stella is in the maternity ward— he sucks on a chicken wing or wolfs down cake. He even eats during one of Blanche's most moving monologues in the script, when she mentions the "beauty of the mind, richness of the spirit, tenderness of the heart" that she has in abundance and that are worth so much more than passing beauty. In the same scene, after having changed in front of Blanche, Stanley sprays his face with beer while laughing. Compared to the evanescent Vivien Leigh, Brando seems a voracious appetite, an unstoppable force; in short, a body that makes its presence felt.

A Repertoire of Gestures

One of Brando's gestures sums up Stanley, with all his power, dangerousness, and erotic appeal. It's the particular way he grabs the arm of the person he's speaking to that is repeated several times over the course of the film. It happens the first time in the scene where Kowalski and Stella fight over Blanche's luggage while she's taking one of her interminable hot baths. Stanley wants to know how the DuBois family's money was spent—who knows, maybe on those ritzy outfits, that jewelry spilling out the trunk? A good question, especially since, according to the Napoleonic Code in force in Louisiana, his wife's inheritance belongs to him as well. But Stella doesn't want to hear her husband's suspicions, or listen to the ugly lure of profit he expresses so shamelessly. She continues to tidy up without paying much attention to him, and two times he grabs her arm to stop her. "Will you listen?" he asks, getting worked up. And he drags her roughly by the arm over to the suspect suitcase—a typical gesture to represent male irritation as well as a man's domination over his wife. Until the scene where Blanche, finally out of the bathroom, finds herself alone with Stanley. Taking advantage of her sister's absence, she tries to charm him with her many flirtatious wiles. A touch from her is all it takes to awaken the wildcat within him: her little tap on the shoulder arouses the rage of Stanley, who yells at her. With a girlish laugh, she insists he admire her dress, light her cigarette, spray perfume on her. That's when Stanley suddenly grabs her arm: "You know, if I didn't know you was my wife's sister I would get ideas about you." What a breakthrough! For we just saw Stanley use this gesture of grabbing the arm a few minutes earlier, and several other times, with Stella. If Blanche acts like a tease, Stanley reacts like he does with his

own wife. We are at the very heart of the taste for ambivalence Kazan passed on to Brando: the dialogue says one thing—here, that Stanley doesn't appreciate his sister-in-law seducing him—while the actor's body speaks to another— a real erotic familiarity with Blanche.

Even before the big scene of Blanche's birthday party, Brando uses his body language to make us believe Stella's line: "Stanley's always smashed things." Yet there are few moments of real violence in the film. The poker scene where he throws the radio out the window; the scene where he clears the table with one sweep of his hand while proclaiming, "Just remember what Huey Long said: that every man's a king and I'm the king around here. And don't you forget it"; when he grasps Blanche the night Stella gives birth to their child. Between these various scenes are long stretches of calm, decidedly worrisome since we're waiting for a swing to the other extreme at any moment. Look at the scene where, unbeknownst to the two sisters, Stanley overhears Blanche going off on the behavior of prehistoric man. "'His Poker night,' you call it. This party of apes?" Afterward, he enters into the room extremely quietly, for once offering Blanche a big smile. Though Stella throws herself on him, he keeps his wry gaze fixed on his sister-in-law. The message is clear and Blanche receives it perfectly: Stanley has won the contest. Present in this scene, his carnal bond with Stella is of course blatant when, after a fight, Stanley makes her come back to him by shouting his famous, "Stella!" Here we see the choreography of the first confrontation between Blanche and her brother-in-law again, but in reverse. This time, it's Stanley who stands facing a female body that approaches him languorously. Stella slowly descends the stairs, and once she's very close, Stanley melodramatically lifts his hand to his heart then drops to his knees. She hugs him to her, and this image of the enraged wildcat tamed at last, finally knocked down, sums up marvelously what Tennessee Williams described tirelessly throughout his work: how much sexuality is both a tremendous force of alienation and the only sincere expression of our profound being.

If the film version of *Streetcar* is a miracle of chemistry between its actors, it's thanks to the Stanley–Stella relationship as well. How striking is the intensity of Kim Hunter and Marlon Brando's intimacy, their understanding that goes beyond words, their familiarity with each other's bodies! These are all things that Tennessee Williams's dialogue expresses: "I can hardly stand it when he's away for a night. […] When he's away for a week I nearly go wild. […] When he comes back… I cry in his lap like a baby," Stella confides to her sister. Later, Blanche becomes indignant, "What you're talking about is desire, just brutal desire. The name of that rattle-trap streetcar that bangs through the Quarter."

With Stella, Stanley is uncouth, of course, but he always makes an unexpected vague gesture of tenderness; at times his voice takes on a gentle lilt. After sweeping Blanche's birthday dinner aside with the back of his hand, there he is, against all expectations, tenderly embracing Stella and kissing her on the neck. The way they complement each other is amazing: she seems to have absorbed his violence, just as he seems to have acquired some of her femininity. When he gives Blanche her return ticket, Stella, furious and wounded, grabs him from behind and rips his shirt with a power, an immediacy that's all Kowalski. "And not only was he ambivalent in his performance, he was ambivalent within himself about who he was as a human being. So you got this richness going on in this movie," notes Richard Schickel.[37] And when Stanley tries to control his temper, calmly bringing his hands together, or when he responds to her passionate kiss at the foot of the stairs, he seems as gentle as a lamb, delicate even, with a face, as Capote says, whose "almost angelic refinement" and expression of "gentleness" stand out in perfect contrast to his "hard-jawed good looks" and "brawny body."[38]

The Rendezvous

The climax of *A Streetcar Named Desire* is of course the rape scene, that inevitable rendezvous between Stanley and Blanche that troubled the censors so much back then. In this bit of bravura, Brando's performance relies on alternating unpredictably between violence and gentleness. To pull Blanche out of her delirium—the twofold fiction of Shep the millionaire's invitation to go on a cruise and Mitch's apology—he throws her brutally onto the bed and screams in her face, "You know what I say? Ha ha! You hear me? Ha ha ha!" This incredible stridency reduces Stanley to a force of pure destruction. The next instant, he's calm and smiling, wearing silk pajamas. When Blanche asks her brother-in-law to let her pass, Stanley kicks in a bit the chair that stands between them: "You've got plenty of room to get by me now." And slowly he moves toward her with a look of bottomless joy. The image turns terrifying as Brando's catlike move-ments, the malicious glint in his eye, become a sign, for us as well as for Blanche, of an uncontrol-lable viciousness, a frightening destructive urge. That's when he struggles with her, attempting to lock her in his arms and avoid the broken bottle with which she vainly tries to defend herself, his body dodging her blows with the agility of a boxer. Think of Edie and Terry's first meeting in *On the Waterfront*—also a fight, but an innocent one. The gestures, the ease, the unmediated sensuality, the malice: the ingredients are the same but their effect is the complete opposite. Except that in the final scene, when—at Stanley's request—a doctor comes to commit Blanche DuBois, there's no

Stella Adler (1901–1992): The daughter of two stars of the Yiddish stage, Adler began her acting career at the age of four. In 1922, filled with enthusiasm by the American tour of the Moscow Art Theater, she found a true acting guru in Constantin Stanislavski (1863–1938), with whom she studied closely in Paris in 1934. Her husband, Harold Clurman, cofounded the avant-garde Group Theatre with Lee Strasberg, but Stella, disagreeing with Strasberg over what constituted an inspired performance, broke with him and left to teach at Erwin Piscator's Dramatic Workshop. There she became Brando's mentor. In 1949, she founded her own school, which today continues to pass down the Adler Method.

Lee Strasberg (1901–1982): Born in a far corner of the Austro-Hungarian Empire, Strasberg belonged to a family of Russian Jews that soon immigrated to New York. He made his acting debut in Yiddish theater and, like Stella Adler, took to his profession with passion when he discovered the theater of Constantin Stanislavski during his 1922 American tour. He then developed a very personal vision of the actor's work, based particularly on the use of emotional or affective memory to fuel a performance. It was on this basis that Strasberg transformed Stanislavski's teachings into an extremely popular "Method" that he taught at the Actors Studio, which he directed from 1951 until his death in 1982.

longer any hint of Stanley's malevolence, the evil
nature that seemed to be revealed at last in the
rape scene. And so he's back to being tender
with Stella, passionate about his poker game,
indifferent to his sister-in-law's fate, yes, but far
from the heartless tormentor of the preceding
scene. Thus Brando leaves us with the fundamental
question: Who is Stanley Kowalski? A sadist
at large, the incarnation of the world's brutality?
Or a nice but somewhat crude guy, a slave to
his urges, who doesn't think about the conse-
quences of his actions? If there is no answer, if
A Streetcar Named Desire continues to fascinate
and test our moral sense, it's thanks to Tennessee
Williams and Elia Kazan, to their brilliant
writing and vivid directing. But it's also thanks
to Marlon Brando—innocent and perverse,
destructive and charming, a shrewd connoisseur
of the human heart in general and of his character
Stanley's in particular.

2   Mark Antony

Julius Caesar (1953)
Joseph L. Mankiewicz

"I come not, friends, to steal away your hearts:
I am no orator, as Brutus is;
But, as you know me all, a plain blunt man,
That love my friend."
— Mark Antony

One fine day during the 1960s, after years of cinematic triumphs and extreme celebrity, Marlon Brando stopped working. Or, more precisely, stopped learning his lines. After all, why memorize pages and pages if you can simply hide a few signs around the set or even stick a Post-it on your costar's forehead? "Yeah, you save all that time not learning the lines," Brando would explain to justify what might well have been nothing more than laziness. "You can't tell the difference. And it improves the spontaneity, because you really don't know. You have an idea of it and you're saying it and you can't remember what the hell it is you want to say. I think it's an aid. Except, of course, Shakespeare. I can quote you two hours of plays and speeches from Shakespeare."[39] Ah, Shakespeare! More than twenty years after playing one of the key roles in *Julius Caesar*, Brando still knew some of its passages by heart.[40] The memory of a motherly maxim repeated ad nauseam: "You haven't done anything until you've done Shakespeare."[41] The afterglow of a bygone era when he would hammer away at preparing for his roles. And, above all, the indelible imprint of his encounter with an exceptional role.

From Stanley Kowalski to Mark Antony

He sure did work hard at his Mark Antony! Never before and never again did Marlon Brando invest himself in this way. Even the great Shakespearean John Gielgud—who played Cassius in Joseph Mankiewicz's version—was astonished. Brando was "a funny, intense, egocentric boy of twenty-seven,"[42] Gielgud noted after meeting the star, who despite his broad shoulders gave "the effect of a lean Greenwich Village college boy. He is very nervous indeed and mutters his lines and rehearses by himself all day long."[43] John Houseman, the film's prestigious producer—he cofounded the Mercury Theatre with Orson Welles—recounts in his memoirs having seen Brando work day and night. It must be said that the young actor was under a hell of a lot of pressure. For someone who

was still a macho factory worker from New Orleans in everyone's mind, choosing to play a Roman patrician caused a stir. On television, during the very popular *Colgate Comedy Hour*, Jerry Lewis had a ball caricaturing Brando as a dull brute, with a jutting jaw and broken syntax. It wasn't just journalists who took him for Stanley Kowalski but everyone he met who was still haunted by *Streetcar*'s atmosphere of muggy sensuality. Tired of the mix-up, Brando took extreme care of his physical appearance, wearing tailored suits and fedoras. It made no difference: critics and audiences reproached him for his speech impediment, that famous unintelligible mumbling that set off alarms in advance of such a prestigious play. And, really, an American performing Shakespeare, doing justice to the play's extremely difficult iambic pentameters—could he pull it off? Of course, Mark Antony isn't the lead role of this tragedy of power in which Brutus and Cassius get top billing, since the play is about the plot to assassinate Caesar and, once the crime is committed, the hunt for the conspirators that ensues.

What did it matter that he was surrounded by skeptics and mockers? Brando got to work. He listened over and over to every recording he could find of the monologues of Mark Antony, notably the famous, "Friends, Romans, countrymen…" (*Julius Caesar*, act III, scene 2), the eulogy that Caesar's shady protégé delivers over the murdered dictator's corpse, performing the miracle of using his oratorical talent to turn a hostile mob. Brando's models? Two venerable Brits: Sir Laurence Olivier, of course, and Sir Ralph Richardson, the former's partner at the Old Vic—both legendary Mark Antonys, the first dazzling with his beauty and intelligence and the second full of seductive cunning. A recording of John Barrymore, another theater legend, also fascinated Brando. Hadn't that great tragedian offered proof that an American could do honor to the language of the Bard? On vacation at his parents' house in Nebraska, Marlon drove everyone crazy by shouting his monologues for hours on end, his mouth pressed against his pillow—he hoped in this way to reproduce the acoustics of the Forum. Despite all his efforts, the first reading went poorly. Intimidated by the presence of the Brits John Gielgud and James

Marlon Brando as Mark Antony in Joseph L. Mankiewicz's *Julius Caesar* (1953).

Mason, Brando made a disastrous impression.
John Houseman recounts: "Brando, who
appeared in a striped sweater with a rolled
umbrella and whom everyone was dying to
hear, gave a perfect performance as a stuttering
bumpkin only remotely acquainted with the
English language."[44]

Finally, after three weeks of rehearsal—an
unusually long time in film—shooting began.
The star started off by approaching John Gielgud
in all his youthful arrogance, questioning his
ability to play a Roman soldier and complaining
about his effeminate bearing. But Brando the
actor was more intelligent than Brando the man.
He accepted the obvious once he watched his
elder in action: John Gielgud was, quite simply,
a tremendous actor, and the beauty of his
performance left no doubt. "No one dared change
the smallest word without my approval," noted
Gielgud sarcastically. "They seemed to imagine
I was in some sort of contact with Shakespeare."[45]
From then on, the young man showed up on set
even when he wasn't shooting to watch the scenes
in which Cassius appeared. He forged a trusting
relationship with Gielgud, even making him
record the Forum monologue to better prepare
for his own role. Flattered, the actor considered
bringing the young prodigy back to England
to play Hamlet, under his direction. But since
he'd discovered the comforts of cinema, Brando
had turned his back on the theater, and he never

returned to it. It mattered little to him that the
great Joseph L. Mankiewicz, an expert since he'd
just portrayed the life of the stage so well in *All
About Eve* (1950), saw in him "the single greatest
acting talent in the English language of this
century [...] better than Clift, better than Orson
and Burton."[46]

Mankiewicz, a New Mentor?

Mankiewicz himself was an essential influence
on Brando's performance. He approached the
Shakespearean classic like "a living drama."[47]
Each actor had to give the impression not of
reciting but of truly coming up with his lines over
the course of the story. And this man of culture
and extreme refinement became a father figure
during a troubled time for Brando. In April 1952,
while he was shooting the great Forum scene,
Marlon learned that Elia Kazan, his mentor,
friend, and long-time protector, had given names
to the House Un-American Activities Commission
(HUAC). A former Communist Party member,[48]
like most of the New York theater community in
the 1930s and '40s, the director had at first refused
to give in to the pressure of Senator McCarthy's
investigators and help them determine which
of his colleagues were or had been communists.
But at his second summoning, he decided to
speak, and to provide names, eight of them: those
of close associates, actor or writer friends...

Opposite: Marlon Brando and Joseph L. Mankiewicz on the set of the film.

Mark Antony standing before Caesar, who has just been assassinated by Cassius and Brutus.

even the name of a dead man. The testimony of this "friendly witness," as they were called at the time, was a bombshell. A beloved theater director and celebrated filmmaker, Kazan had everything needed to resist the destructive atmosphere of the "witch hunt." His action was perceived by the Hollywood community as an unacceptable betrayal, as the "arrangement"[49] of an unscrupulous opportunist.

For his part, Mankiewicz, likewise at the pinnacle of his success—*All About Eve* had just won six Oscars!—was a die-hard anti-McCarthyist. President of the Screen Directors Guild in 1950–1951, he was confronted with a fierce anti-communist offensive led by the director Cecil B. DeMille, who used Mankiewicz's absence from a meeting to attempt to pass a resolution by the Board of Directors aimed at excluding any former or current communists from the Guild. Upon his return, Mankiewicz convoked a general assembly and gave an indignant speech in which he called for breathing "the air of liberty in a dramatic manner." Directors as prestigious as John Ford, William Wyler, Fritz Lang, Josef von Sternberg, and Douglas Sirk were in attendance. That day, Mankiewicz got his revenge by forcing the Board to resign.[50] Which is to say that the day Brando's emotional world collapsed, the actor, disappointed by Kazan, was able to turn to his director in *Julius Caesar* without worry. Confronted with Brando and his distress, Mankiewicz felt helpless: "I mean,

what do you say to somebody whose father has just died?"[51]

From then on, Brando sought Mankiewicz out for advice about every detail in his life: performance, private life, choice of a doctor or psychoanalyst… It was a way of reproducing his relationship with Kazan and constructing a link that would barely endure beyond the two films they shot together (*Julius Caesar* then *Guys and Dolls*). After having bothered everyone during the rehearsals for *Julius Caesar* with his eccentricities and his incomprehensible diction, during the shooting Brando revealed his brilliant talent and perfect English. On soundstage 24 of MGM Studios, where the recent set of *Quo Vadis* (Mervyn LeRoy, 1951) had been recycled as a Forum, the extras and the film crew thunderously applauded his "Friends, Romans, countrymen, lend me your ears!" Mankiewicz himself was delighted. "During the whole rehearsal period with Marlon Brando, when we were alone, I kept having trouble with the same phrase. At the beginning of his speech, Mark Antony says, 'Friends, lend me your ears' and I asked myself, why doesn't he just say 'Listen to me.' […] For the shooting of the scene, we had three hundred extras. I told them to act not like extras but like actors who were playing the role of Roman citizens: I asked them to really pay attention to what James Mason was going to tell them in his role as Brutus. During the rehearsal, Brutus's speech moved them so much that when Brando arrived, carrying Caesar's corpse in his arms, the crowd groaned and started to shout: the citizens of Rome refused to hear what Mark Antony had to tell them. At that moment, I understood what Shakespeare wanted to say. He knew that the Romans would not listen to Mark Antony and that he would have to ask them to be silent. 'Lend me your ears.' Mark Antony could not have said it differently. This extraordinary emotion of discovery that I just had I owe to my encounter with the great actor Marlon Brando and that unique writer, Shakespeare."[52] Mankiewicz's enthusiasm was largely shared when the movie was released. The harsh Bosley Crowther raved in the *New York Times*, "Next to Mr. Gielgud's Cassius, the delight and surprise of the film is Mr. Brando's Mark Antony, which is something memorable to see. Athletic and bullet-headed, he looks the realest Roman of them all and possesses the fire of hot convictions and the firm elasticity of steel. Happily, Mr. Brando's diction, which has been guttural and slurred in previous films, is clear and precise in this instance. In him a major talent has emerged."[53] Mankiewicz himself was so excited about his actor that he sent him a telegram, because a few months after *Julius Caesar* he was starting his new project, the musical comedy *Guys and Dolls* (1955). Mankiewicz hoped that Brando would accept the role of Sky Masterson. Insofar as he would write the part for Brando, he said, it would constitute as much as a challenge as playing Mark Antony. "Understand you're apprehensive because you've never done musical comedy. You have nothing repeat nothing to worry about. Because neither have I."[54] They hadn't done Shakespeare before, either, but Mankiewicz was certain that the experience of filming a musical comedy would be every bit as exciting and gratifying.

The Realest Roman of Them All

How did Brando manage to win over the mob of skeptics? Bosley Crowther gives us a clue when he raves about Brando being "the realest Roman of them all." It's true that with his aquiline nose and his athletic chest, the star had the profile of a Roman coin and the body of a statue. Just as much as in *A Streetcar Named Desire*, Brando was filmed in *Julius Caesar* as a sex symbol, though not only in the hope of luring young female fans into movie halls. As the fashion of the time dictated, together Houseman and Mankiewicz decided to reinforce the political allegory of Shakespeare's play with allusions to contemporary history: Caesar's Rome clearly evokes Nazi Germany and the fall of the dictator the Allied victory. The opening credits roll over a flag depicting a menacing eagle—which inevitably evokes the imagery of the Third Reich. The eagle then becomes a leitmotif. It's found

on a servant's tunic, on the brooch Caesar uses to close his toga just before the Ides of March, and finally on Caesar's chair that Mark Antony takes in a key scene, a wordless addition to the Shakespearean text. The mob that listens to Mark Antony's harangue at the Forum, at first hostile and then moved, cries in unison and holds up arms in a gesture that deliberately recalls the fascist salute. "Since Antony is about to 'unleash the dogs of war,' the scene may even have carried overtones, at least in some viewers' minds, of the infamous moment in February of 1942 when Joseph Goebbels had asked the German people amassed in the Berlin Sportpalast, 'Do you want total war?' Mankiewicz's Roman mob is as susceptible to demagoguery as the mob in Nazi Germany," notes Martin M. Winkler.[55] In this context, the carefully highlighted attractiveness of Mark Antony—notably in the scene of the Forum where he's glistening with sweat—is also a way of associating the character with fascism, with its ideal of virility and strength, and its intermingling ideology and aesthetics.

We might object that all of this results single-handedly from the skill of the director. Except that Brando, in perfect harmony with Mankiewicz, uses this political dimension nicely to fuel his performance. Take, for example, the scene between Antony and Octavius that closely follows the funeral oration for Caesar. Mark Antony, the warrior, obviously dominates: he moves with ease, sitting on the desk while Octavius, seated, immobile, is but a passive presence. When the latter finally leaves the room, the camera stays on Mark Antony, who advances onto the terrace overlooking Rome, stretches out his arms, turns toward the bust of Caesar, and smiles at it. In a film of such extreme fidelity to the original work, here's a rare moment that neither John Gielgud nor James Mason could get from their director: a moment where, going beyond the text, the camera lingers on a silent actor. "With that statue, it was just two silent looks… like a passage of exquisite music," Mankiewicz recalled, decidedly transported.[56] In this brief moment, Brando demonstrates with great precision the ambiguity of Shakespeare's character—while the parallel with the Third Reich, though undeniably powerful, risks a lack of subtlety. In the play, Mark Antony epitomizes the temptation of demagoguery: isn't the Forum scene a terrifying demonstration of the people's inconstancy? "Here the funeral oration is nothing but a pretext," explains François-Victor Hugo, a French translator of Shakespeare, in his preface to the play. "In reality, it is not Caesar's glory that must be defended, it is the cause of Caesarism itself. Will society be free or enslaved? Will it be governed by principles or controlled by force? Will it be a republic or will it be an empire? That is the question. Whether the people vindicate Brutus, and the republic is saved. Or whether they

Marlon Brando makes the cover of *Life* (April 20, 1953) for his role as Mark Antony in *Julius Caesar*.

LIFE

MARLON BRANDO AS ANTONY
IN MOVIE, 'JULIUS CAESAR'

20 CENTS

APRIL 20, 1953

REG. U. S. PAT. OFF.

35

Opposite: Marlon Brando
rehearsing the scene
of the monologue on the steps
of the Forum.

Mark Antony stands before the
people of Rome to offer a final
funeral oration for Caesar.

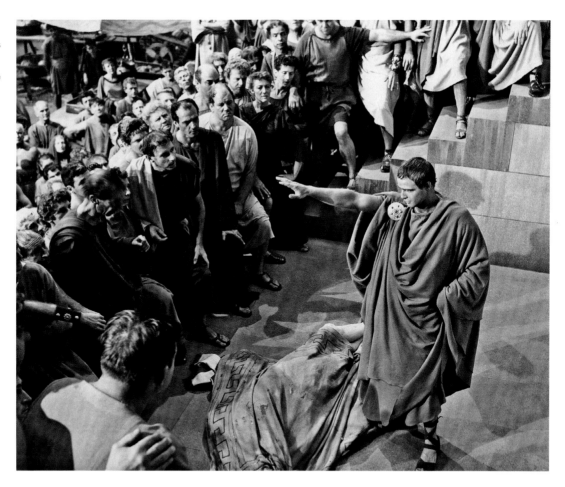

side with Antony, and the empire is built. Caesar's bloody mantle must be the sinister shroud of liberty." His appetite for power and his skillful manipulation of the mob make it understood that Mark Antony is a tyrant in the making and that to follow his law would be to turn away from the ideal of a just and measured form of governance. But far from being detestable, the character instead earns the audience's respect. We admire his loyalty to Caesar and his memory, his desire to avenge a man who has been betrayed by those close to him, notably by Brutus, his adoptive son, who sacrificed him for Rome's greater interest. The appearances of Caesar's ghost and the misfortune that descends upon the characters— Brutus and Cassius end up taking their own lives —suggest that the murder was not an irreproachable act of civic-mindedness. Those who committed it incur divine retribution.

In his short silent scene, Brando summarizes this dramatic sophistication perfectly. His freedom of movement suggests his appetite for power, his physical strength an ardent desire for conquest. The look he gives Caesar's bust, the way he smiles at it, expresses the love he had for his spiritual father. We touch on a crucial theme of the play here, where the emotional ties among men constantly compete with political concerns. Yet it's Brando's final gesture that gives the scene its full weight: he sits in Caesar's chair to reread the deceased's will, an instrument he's used with virtuoso skill to

win over the mob in the Forum scene. The image sums up all the complexity of a character possibly moved by an almost filial piety, but also thirsty for power, profoundly relieved to have finally emerged from the shadow of the great man and now free to take his place. The scene opens a horizon, one on which Mark Antony's destiny can play out, one Shakespeare recounted in another of his Roman tragedies, *Antony and Cleopatra* (circa 1606), and which Richard Burton performed superbly for Mankiewicz in *Cleopatra* (1963).

From the beginning of the film, when we first see Mark Antony walking behind Caesar among the members of the procession during the Lupercalia, he appears peculiar and solitary: filmed mostly in profile, a borrowing from Christian iconography that suggests guile —like Judas, he avoids eye contact —he's always distinctly detached from the group. The full meaning of this positioning becomes clear when Caesar is murdered and Antony enters the Senate, where he discovers the conspirators, who have just bathed their hands in their victim's blood. Mark Antony goes straight to Caesar's corpse, his eyes downcast, ignoring those who surround him:
O mighty Caesar! dost thou lie so low?
Are all thy conquests, glories, triumphs, spoils,
Shrunk to this little measure? Fare thee well.
The sincere grief and unaffected nobility imprinted on his face and in his voice earns the trust of the murderers—at the very least, Brutus' —as well as

the viewer's. A moment later, Mark Antony asks
to shake the conspirators' hands:
Let each man render me his bloody hand:
First, Marcus Brutus, will I shake with you;
Next, Caius Cassius, do I take your hand;
Now, Decius Brutus, yours: now yours, Metellus;
Yours, Cinna; and, my valiant Casca, yours;
Though last, not last in love, yours, good
Trebonius.[57]
And in fact, Mark Antony shakes each man's hand.
After the last, he looks at his own hand, as if to
verify that it's not stained with blood — a silent
accusation of rare power and a choice that allows
Brando to suggest the dichotomy between what
Antony says, his apparent warmth, his decla-
rations of affection, and what he really thinks of
Caesar's assassins.

The Power of the Tribune

At last we come to the great scene of the funeral
oration. It is the only moment of the film where
Brando speaks loudly and goes so far as to
shout — in other words, the only moment where
he acts as if he's on stage. The reason for this is
quite simple: at this point, Mark Antony has an
audience and he knows it, as is immediately
shown, just before the beginning of the speech,
by the close-up of his lowered face, as he tunes
in to the mood of the crowd. Mankiewicz's
direction underscores just how powerful the

tribune is at this moment in the film: the camera
tracks all his movements and uses a subtle balance
between high- and low-angle shots to emphasize
his influence on the assembly he overlooks.
The scene therefore seems to be a metaphor for
the power an actor holds over his audience.
Antony recalls, with consummate attention to
detail, the cruelty of Caesar's fate:
Look, in this place ran Cassius' dagger through:
See what a rent the envious Casca made:
Through this the well-beloved Brutus stabb'd;
And as he pluck'd his cursed steel away,
Mark how the blood of Caesar follow'd it.
His words and the conviction he puts into
pronouncing them evoke images, stir emotions.
The effect is immediate: "O, now you weep,"
he exclaims, a line that Brando punctuates with
an ironic, cruel smile befitting the play that
François-Victor Hugo called "a masterpiece of
political perfidy." Far be it from us to question
this passionate vehemence, this eloquently worded
grief… until that irresistible smile, slipped in by
Brando at just the right moment. For it reminds
us, if we've allowed ourselves to be carried away
by emotion, that this harangue is above all an
exercise in control. Self-control and control of
his gestures. Control of others and their feelings.
"Now let it work. Mischief, thou art afoot.
Take thou what course thou wilt!" concludes
Antony in an aside cut from the film, reveling in
the anger he has aroused among the Romans.

Marlon Brando finally tackles
Shakespeare by playing
Mark Antony.

Opposite and following pages:
Mark Antony addresses the
Romans vehemently after
Caesar's murder.

Friends, Romans, countrymen, lend me your ears;
I come to bury Caesar, not to praise him.
The evil that men do lives after them;
The good is oft interred with their bones;
So let it be with Caesar. The noble Brutus
Hath told you Caesar was ambitious:
If it were so, it was a grievous fault,
And grievously hath Caesar answer'd it.
Here, under leave of Brutus and the rest—
For Brutus is an honourable man;
So are they all, all honourable men—
Come I to speak in Caesar's funeral.
He was my friend, faithful and just to me:
But Brutus says he was ambitious;
And Brutus is an honourable man.
He hath brought many captives home to Rome
Whose ransoms did the general coffers fill:
Did this in Caesar seem ambitious?
When that the poor have cried, Caesar hath wept:
Ambition should be made of sterner stuff:
Yet Brutus says he was ambitious;
And Brutus is an honourable man.
You all did see that on the Lupercal
I thrice presented him a kingly crown,
Which he did thrice refuse: was this ambition?
Yet Brutus says he was ambitious;
And, sure, he is an honourable man.
I speak not to disprove what Brutus spoke,
But here I am to speak what I do know.
You all did love him once, not without cause:

What cause withholds you then, to mourn for him?
O judgment! thou art fled to brutish beasts,
And men have lost their reason. Bear with me;
My heart is in the coffin there with Caesar,
And I must pause till it come back to me.

Even more than the death of Caesar, it is the words of Mark Antony—carefully chosen, magnificently declaimed—that accelerate the drama. At this moment, Antony gets ahold of a precious instrument, Caesar's will, which he will brandish at an opportune moment. Let's not forget that Antony feigns spontaneity: the will is too obvious and too visible an addendum; if he were to let himself wave it too much under the mob's noses, they would suspect him of manipulation. Likewise, his eyes barely glance at the document, as if to suggest in passing that he knows it by heart. At last comes his wild cry, "Here was a Caesar! When comes such another?" Leaving the Romans to their rage, Mark Antony turns his back to them and steps up toward the camera, a slight smile on his lips. The smile of the tribune who knows he's won the battle. The smile as well of a young actor who has won the crowd over, silenced the skeptics, and henceforth reigns supreme in world cinema.

Terry Malloy

On the Waterfront (1954)
Elia Kazan

"They always said I was a bum. Well, I ain't a bum, Edie. Don't worry, I'm not gonna hurt nobody. I'm just gonna go down there and get my rights."
—Terry Malloy

What if Terry Malloy had Paul Newman's blue eyes? Or the warm voice of Frank Sinatra? When casting began for *On the Waterfront*, Elia Kazan and Marlon Brando hadn't spoken for several months. The star had experienced his spiritual father's cooperation with the House Un-American Activities Commission as an unforgivable betrayal.[58] He still felt an anger and mistrust of him that no conversation or friendly intervention managed to ease. And to further complicate matters, Kazan, foul-tempered and big-headed, also held a grudge against Brando: who was this cocky kid to dare criticize anything at all about the man who gave him everything? Wasn't Brando his discovery? His Stanley Kowalski, his Emiliano Zapata? Would it be up to him, the Pygmalion, to make the first gesture of reconciliation toward his creature? Unthinkable! Better to gamble on a new discovery, uncover another acting genius. It's not so difficult. Besides, as luck would have it, there happened to be a real Greek god at the Actors Studio by the name of Paul Newman. As Kazan wrote his producer Sam Spiegel, Newman had it in him to be "a really wonderful prospect, handsome, rugged, sexy and somehow turbulent inside…" Not to mention he "looks quite a lot like Brando."[59] After all, who said Terry Malloy was a role for Marlon Brando?

Sinatra or Brando

Terry's a little guy from Hoboken, New Jersey. A brainless "good-for-nothing" easily manipulated by his brother Charley and Johnny Friendly, the local godfather. And in a happy coincidence, Hoboken was the birthplace of a first-rate star, an unassuming runt whose blue eyes were immediately likable: Frank Sinatra. While Kazan polished the script with his partner, Budd Schulberg, Sam Spiegel, a true Hollywood legend, with his humble beginnings, his cigar sticking out of his mouth, and his camel-hair coat, organized negotiations with "The Voice." "For Chrissakes, you are Hoboken!" he told the singer while giving him

a big slap on the back.[60] Sinatra was beside himself. For the past several years, his stormy marriage to Ava Gardner and his vocal-cord problems had led him irresistibly to film, a real miracle cure for a failing career. The singer had just brilliantly pulled off a supporting role in *From Here to Eternity* (1953). And here came a leading role in Hoboken, on his own turf, under the direction of the greatest filmmaker of the time. Had the luck of "Frankie Blue Eyes" finally turned around?

That's not taking into account Sam Spiegel, a man of a thousand tricks. While courting Sinatra, he engaged Brando in talks. Brando let him beg a long time before accepting the unbeatable argument: "Politics has nothing to do with this— it's about your talent, it's about your career."[61] So Brando agreed to read Budd Schulberg's script. He soon accepted the obvious: he was Terry Malloy. Sinatra took the news pretty badly. "One day," his valet recounted, "I arrived to see the living room half destroyed. Two lamps had been knocked over, broken glass was covering the floor. At first I thought there had been a burglary, until I began cleaning up and found the remnants of several drafts of a script entitled *On the Waterfront* by Budd Schulberg. […] I found Mr. S in bed nursing several bad paper cuts on his hands, which he got ripping up the script. He apologized for flipping out and told me he had just lost the role of a lifetime and that he had been fucked over by the worst real Sammy Glick[62] in the business, Sammy Spiegel. […] Then he went into a tirade against Sam Spiegel that lasted for the next couple of weeks."[63] Meanwhile, Brando set his terms: he wanted a big advance instead of a percentage of the box office receipts—a glaring error that the film's success would make him bitterly regret. And above all, he demanded to be done with filming by three o'clock for his daily session on the couch of his New York analyst, Dr. Mittelman. The whim of an arrogant star? The expression of deep suffering going back to childhood? Both perhaps. To which we must add: a message intended for Elia Kazan, a sign that all was not forgiven, that Marlon was no longer the malleable young man from *Streetcar* and that, if he was influenced by anyone, it was now by his therapist.

Yet, for Elia Kazan, *On the Waterfront* was a profoundly personal film, a work whose

Marlon Brando makes himself up to play Terry Malloy in Elia Kazan's *On the Waterfront* (1954).

45

Marlon Brando, Elia Kazan, and Eva Marie Saint on the set of *On the Waterfront*.

Opposite, top: Arthur Marotta, Hoboken's public safety director, Elia Kazan, Marlon Brando and Boris Kaufman, the film's director of photography.

Opposite, bottom: Terry Malloy (Marlon Brando) is still under the control of his brother, Charley Malloy (Rod Steiger), and of Johnny Friendly (Lee J. Cobb), the local mob boss.

Following pages: Terry Malloy, a little guy from New Jersey, grapples with the waterfront mob.

intimate charge exploded in each shot. At first, the man whose friends nicknamed him Gadg (for Gadget) started to write his drama of the dock mobsters with Arthur Miller, his best friend, obsessed like him with paternal relationships and driven by a strong social conscience. Except that Kazan's testimony—always that!—had caused a long falling out with the playwright, with whom he had created the Broadway masterpiece *Death of a Salesman*. Kazan therefore allied himself with Budd Schulberg, who was himself working on a similar project entitled "The Bottom of the River". There was no chance Schulberg would hold a grudge against Kazan for his McCarthyist connections: instead of waiting for his summons, this son of a Paramount producer who had grown up in the film world went of his own accord before the House Un-American Activities Commission on May 23, 1951, long enough to give a deposition consisting of a violent indictment against the Communist Party.[64] Thus it was working together that Schulberg and Kazan endowed their story with the theme of corruption and used it to denounce a personal experience that haunted them both, and that still made them feel guilty, though they hardly admitted it. Schulberg would later deny the allegorical character of *On the Waterfront*. But Kazan, always frank, would readily admit, "When Brando, at the end, yells at Lee Cobb, the mob boss, 'I'm glad what I done—you hear

me?—glad what I done!' that was me saying, with identical heat, that I was glad I'd testified as I had. I'd been snubbed by friends each and every day for many months in my old show business haunts, and I'd not forgotten nor would I forgive the men, old friends some of them, who'd snubbed me, so the scene in the film where Brando goes back to the waterfront to 'shape up' again for employment and is rejected by men with whom he'd worked day after day—that, too, was my story, now told to all the world."[65] A sentiment that smoldered all the more since among those "old friends" whose "snubs" Kazan would not forgive was his very own leading man, Marlon Brando.

A Young Boxer Under the Thumb

Once he'd accepted the role, Brando proved fairly cooperative. Without complaining too much, he put up with the rough conditions of shooting in freezing temperatures and a hostile environment—the real local mafia, concerned that the film was a little too realistic, kept a close eye on the set. Brando's first appearance on the screen is somewhat surprising. With swollen eyes and a split eyebrow, the actor no longer has any of the patrician handsomeness of *Julius Caesar*. He's got a boxer's mug battered by punches and life's misfortunes. That Terry is a fighter, a regular and even a virtuoso in the

Terry Malloy falls in love with Edie Doyle (Eva Marie Saint) after having been involved in the death of the young woman's brother.

ring, is apparent at each instant of Brando's performance. His neck is drawn in between his shoulders, his fists are in his pockets, and he has a spring in his step. If his physical bearing seems so right, it's because he trained with a retired lightweight, Roger Donoghue. The boxer told Peter Manso: "Whenever I'd vary my footwork, he noticed it right away. He enjoyed throwing combinations, and I showed him how to move his left ankle before dragging his right foot so he'd always be on-balance. He was terrific, but I realized he was always studying me."[66] In fact, Brando's footwork in the film is admirable, light and elegant, particularly in the scenes on the roof and in the dark streets of Hoboken when he responds to that sinister call: "Your brother's down here! He wants to see you!" The graceful-ness of his running not only indicates professional training but corresponds as well to the profound nature of the character, sensitive beneath the tough-guy look. In other scenes in the film, Terry demonstrates the techniques of a true boxer: he mimes a match with the kid, a member of the Golden Warriors who tends his pigeon house, then in front of the policeman who once saw him fight and asks him about his tactics at the time. When the young Edie (Eva Marie Saint) tries to snatch from him the metal token that will allow her father to get into the warehouse, he pretends to fight, but doesn't take a single hit, nicely demonstrating his dodging skills. Later, at the bar with her, he sums up his "philosophy of life" with an expressive jabbing gesture: "Do it to him before he does it to you." And when he finally dares to confess to Edie the fatal role he played in the death of her brother Joey and, over-whelmed, she dashes away, Terry, staying behind, wavers slightly, like a boxer one second before the KO. Brando's body expresses with a rare intensity that moment of pure pain.

Paradoxically, Terry's physical strength and his boxing talent render him more vulnerable to those around him—Charley (Rod Steiger), Johnny Friendly (Lee J. Cobb), and their band of suspicious-looking gangsters. The first shot of the film, set to the spectacular music of Leonard Bernstein, shows a small group leaving a shack built on the wharf, overshadowed by a huge ocean liner. Behind his older brother, Terry goes with the flow. Then Charley sends him on a mission, slaps his cheek, and then pushes him by the arm. And Terry obediently goes off, with his odd staggering stride, to lure Joey into a trap. Everything in these first images indicates that Terry is a man under the thumb, whose body can be manipulated at will. What's more, in the scene where the waterfront mobsters are at the bar gathered around their boss, it's obvious that Johnny Friendly considers Terry his property. When Johnny invites him to count money, saying, "It's good for you. Develops your mind," another gangster jokes, "What mind?" Johnny then

defends Terry, praising his boxing exploits: he leans over the young man's shoulders, marking his words with a big slap on the back. In short, Terry the simpleton belongs body and soul to the unfriendly Johnny Friendly. It's only with Edie, who doesn't view him as a boxer but as a guy from the neighborhood, a friend of her brother's, that Terry will free himself from this bondage. *On the Waterfront* is the first in a long series of films with Marlon Brando to tell the story of redemption through love.

Redemption Through Love

And have there ever been more beautiful love scenes than those in *On the Waterfront*? Everything starts after the meeting organized by Father Barry (Karl Malden) at the church is interrupted by Friendly's goons. Terry and Edie find themselves alone, talking in front of the church. "Which side are you with?" asks the girl. "Me? I'm with me, Terry," responds Malloy, with a shrug of his shoulders and a smile as charming as it is egotistical. A bum intervenes who recalls having seen Terry in the area on the night of Joey's murder. Terry, annoyed, shoves him to chase him off. But he doesn't express any real violence: the contrast with his body language in *A Streetcar Named Desire* has never been more pronounced. Terry follows Edie, asking her questions about her education at the convent. It's then that she drops her glove—inadvertently, said Eva Marie Saint. He picks it up, pretends to pluck dirt off of it, settles onto a swing while continuing to ask her questions, and puts the glove on. A brilliant idea, beyond the improvisational genius it reveals: on one hand, it explains the turnaround of the situation—at first Terry was following Edie; now it's the reverse—since Edie, too timid to ask for her glove back, finds herself obliged to stay. On the other hand, it represents, with undeniable symbolic force, Terry's amorous desire for the girl. As for the two characters' movements, they follow a veritable choreography of seduction. Every gesture of the one is reflected in the attitude of the other. Thus, when Edie makes as if to leave, Terry gets off his swing and accompanies her. He leans against a tree trunk to tell her that when she was little she was "a mess," with her braids and braces: "I just mean to tell you that you…" —he stops, shrugs his shoulders, and makes a face—"you grew up very nice." She moves away once more, and here again he follows her. "You don't remember me, do you?" "I remembered you the first moment I saw you." "By the nose, huh?" he replies, letting us admire his profile as he grins. He ends up asking if he can see her again. She wants to know why. He shrugs his shoulders, stares off into space. But as soon as she looks away, he devours her with his eyes.

The result of this long scene, which shows the beginning of a love with admirable delicacy, is

that we know Edie's telling the truth when she confides to her father that Terry's expression reveals he's not a hoodlum like the others. What might be nothing but the delirium of infatuation is in fact a profound truth that only a woman in love can discern. Later, Edie and Terry are in a bar, where he wants to get her to try her first beer. But she can't take part in the game of innocent flirting. She's thinking only of her murdered brother and the guilty ones who are still on the loose, and she begs him, "Help me if you can, for God's sakes." Brando's face shows an insurmountable grief. He can't help her; he is the cause of her despair, and he can't stand it. He pleads with her, "No, no, listen. Don't go. I got my whole life to drink." And he asks forgiveness:
"You're sore at me…"
"What for?" Edie replies.
"Well, you know, for not—not being no help to you."
"You would if you could…"
She strokes his face and leaves the table. Terry, on the verge of tears, rubs his brow. Touching his face is practically an acting tic with Brando, a gesture he lends to all his characters, charging it with various meanings. In *On the Waterfront*, the body language indicates a growing frailty, an overwhelming emotion. For example, in the cab scene, when Charley turns against him, Terry touches his cheek and chin, then lets out an exclamation of wounded astonishment at the idea of his own brother threatening him. But let's return to the bar. Brando, through his facial expression, the devouring look he gives Edie, in short, with the simplest gesture, expresses with all his being Terry's guilt, heightened even more by love. Grasping that he's connected to Friendly's gang, she leaves the bar understanding why "everybody calls you a bum" and leaves Terry in shock, his face devastated by suffering. The physical link between them is what brings this pain: during their next meeting, when Edie discovers Terry lying on the roof, she lays her head on his chest, and he moves his hands slowly, delicately, strokes her hair, and kisses her. The tenderness of this scene has its counterpoint in the one where, after having learned of his role in Joey's death, Edie pounds his chest with her fists before yielding to his kiss.

When Virility and Femininity Become One

The mixture of femininity and virility that makes Marlon Brando unique finds its perfect expression for the first time in the role of Terry Malloy. With his square shoulders and the energy that emanates naturally from him, the actor embodies an ideal of man as a brute, or an "animal," as it's described in the dialogue of *On the Waterfront*, exactly like in *A Streetcar Named Desire*. When he wants to send a cop and his sidekick packing, he tells the two men, "So why don't you and your girlfriend

just take off?" Another example of Brando's brilliant delivery that sums up the "little jab" aspect of the character marvelously. Despite this, his own repertoire of gestures is feminine— the nimbleness of his movements, the tenderness of his gestures—as is the tone of his voice when he finds his pigeons slaughtered, a punishment the Golden Warriors kid inflicts on him for testifying. Back at work after having revealed in court the truth about Joey's death, Terry is the only longshoreman present not to be called up by the foreman. He remains standing there, patiently waiting, his fists in his pockets, with a light sway also found in the bar scene where Father Barry convinces him to give up the idea of killing Friendly. Adding to the feminine register, there are also certain exaggerated movements that belong to the domain of melodrama, like the emphatic hand gesture that underscores Terry's pleading when he forces Edie's door open, after the revelation of his role in Joey's death. Feminine, that's how Terry appeared from the beginning of the film because he was a passive body that brutal men manipulated at will. But he must give free rein, in the scenes with Eva Marie Saint, to a hypersensitive emotionality for this femininity to become a strength. His chemistry with the actress, who at age thirty was making her cinematic debut, accounts for much of the film's success. "In my first scene, I was there with Marlon on the rooftop and we were supposed to kiss. Kazan was talking to me as he always talks with his actors, very quietly, telling me, 'Now you're terrified, Eva. You're a Catholic girl, you're not used to seeing men at night.' I was thinking to myself, 'Gadg, you don't have to tell me a thing about being frightened. I'm so petrified I'm about to run out of here.'"[67] But Brando and Eva Saint Marie got along swimmingly, to the point of showing up together in Hoboken each day of the shoot. "Whatever Kazan saw that convinced him to cast me, Marlon had provoked it in me. I would have had to work for weeks with another actor to get what we got, because like Kazan, he knew how to touch certain buttons,"[68] the future Hitchcock blonde emphasized.

The Confrontation in the Cab

This sensitivity is found again in the famous cab scene, that great confrontation between Terry and Charley, which contains some of the most famous lines in the history of cinema. Budd Schulberg recounted how much Brando dreaded this part of the script, finding it implausible that Terry should hold forth so eloquently—"I could've had class. I could've been a contender. I could've been somebody. Instead of a bum, which is what I am, let's face it"—while his own brother points a pistol at him. To this objection, Kazan responded that Brando had only to push the gun away. Good advice, even if he didn't anticipate the gentleness

Elia Kazan and Marlon Brando on the set of Elia Kazan's *Viva Zapata!* (1952).

Elia Kazan (1909–2003)

When he chose Marlon Brando—whom he directed with Harold Clurman in Maxwell Anderson's *Truckline Cafe*—to play the film version of Stanley Kowalski, Elia Kazan was a successful director, but not yet a legend. The year 1947, when he staged Arthur Miller's *Death of a Salesman* and Tennessee Williams's *Streetcar*, was decisive. There's a production photo from *Viva Zapata!* (1952), the second film Brando and Kazan did together, that perfectly sums up their relationship at the time: the two bare-chested men stand side by side, but Kazan, relaxed and warm, looks at the camera while Brando, completely dependent on his director, looks at him. The trouble between them would begin shortly afterward, when Kazan testified before the House Un-American Activities Committee (see page 30).

Brando accepted the role of Terry Malloy in *On the Waterfront* (1954), but was extremely angry with his mentor… To the point of subsequently refusing the numerous roles Kazan offered him in films ranging from *East of Eden* (1955) to *The Arrangement* (1969). In regard to the latter film—in which Kirk Douglas played the leading role—Kazan wrote in his autobiography: "All Marlon would have to do was come and be photographed; you could have read the part on his face."[a] The filmmaker would never shake the regret he felt for having lost his favorite actor.

With his kindly appearance and his big, comic-book nose, Karl Malden had what you'd call a mug. Born into a family of Serbian descent in Chicago, his love of theater led him to New York, where he joined the Group Theatre with the idea of becoming, in his words, "number one in the number two parts." From the start, his career was intimately connected to Brando's: the two men shared billing in *Truckline Cafe* and *A Streetcar Named Desire*, then in *On the Waterfront* and *One-Eyed Jacks*. However, it was without Brando that he found his finest role: that of Archie Lee, husband of the virginal Baby Doll in the 1956 film of the same name, based on a screenplay by Tennessee Williams and brought to life by Elia Kazan. Later, Malden would make a comeback on television in the series *The Streets of San Francisco* (1972–1977), in which he played Michael Douglas's mentor. "Every time I worked with him, he made me look better," Malden told Larry King the day his friend Brando died.

of Terry's gesture and the accompanying shake
of his head. "Charley… Oh, Charley… Wow,"
he protests, almost tenderly. The reproach is
whispered, the anger murmured. When Charley
causes violence to surge up between them, Terry
responds with love. Fraternal love, or even filial
love, which makes his disappointment that much
greater and revives the tragic memory of the
rigged fight that put an end to his boxing career.
"You was my brother. You should've looked out
for me a little bit," he reminds Charley, tapping
him on the shoulder. The gentleness of his tone
cuts like a knife. This whole scene lends added
force to the one where Terry finds Charley dead
in the street, hung on a wall by the waterfront
mobsters. He slowly, lovingly pulls him down
and casts a wandering grieving gaze over the
body of his much beloved brother. No need for
dialogue: we know everything, after the cab scene,
of the bond that united Terry and Charley and
of the devastating loss the younger and more
fragile of the Malloy brothers has just suffered.

Commented on ad nauseam, the cab scene is
surprising from the start, before Charley even
pulls out his revolver and Terry surprises him
by gently pushing him away. We see Terry getting
into the cab—obviously the backseat of a car
filmed in the studio. Nothing can be seen out the
back window, which is covered with blinds,
and only some very unnatural lights on the faces
of the two actors signal that the cab is moving.

When Charley says he wants to talk to him,
Terry replies, "Nobody ever stopped you from
talking, Charley," with a grin and a gentle teasing
that perfectly sums up the depth of his fraternal
affection. Charley wants to make him understand
that he's wrong to associate with Edie Doyle
and doubt Johnny Friendly. He talks about the
ambition he should nurture, and Terry replies,
"I always figured I'd live a little bit longer without
it." The line and the pride that emanates from
Brando as he says it show that the alleged stupidity
of Terry, that brainless good-for-nothing, was
nothing but a fiction. Charley gets annoyed when
Terry tries to explain to him what he wanted to
show: "There's a lot more to this whole thing than
I thought." The second part of the scene, after
Charley's threat, results from the perfection of
the performance in this introduction. And it's not
hard at all to believe the account of the actress
Barbara Baxley, who remembered Brando being
pale during the filming of *On the Waterfront*.
"What he meant was using all of yourself to have
the emotions of the character. He was saying that
he just wasn't picking it up anymore, having it
ready and on the button. It was draining away
from him, and he felt he was having to go deeper.
He was talking about the kind of energy he thought
he had left […]. He kept repeating: 'I don't know
how I'm going to do this.'"[69]

Incidentally, during the first screening of the
film, Brando got up and left the room. He found

Father Barry (Karl Malden) and Edie come to the aid of Terry, left for dead by Johnny Friendly at the harbor in Hoboken.

Opposite: After getting roughed up by Johnny Friendly, Terry manages to pick himself up to defend his honor.

his performance dreadfully bad. Furious, Kazan had to scream at Spiegel (who began to apologize to Leonard Bernstein), "This film is great!" In fact, the recognition that Brando gained from *On the Waterfront* would surpass the success of *Streetcar*. He won his first Oscar for Best Actor, which he accepted—this time—with enthusiasm.[70] And most of all, the public thronged the movie halls to see Terry Malloy triumph over corruption and general hostility. At the end of the film, Terry is beaten up by Johnny Friendly and his goons, who leave him for dead in the dirty water of the harbor. Inspired by the words of Edie and Father Barry, Terry gets back up and walks to the warehouse, his face disfigured, like Christ during the Stations of the Cross—he even stumbles three times. Kazan's greatness was in knowing how to transform his own story, so inglorious, into universal catharsis. But it was also Brando's genius to make Terry Malloy into a being who is so seemingly vulnerable, so profoundly good, that his triumph over Evil galvanizes each viewer and overcomes all resistance.

4 Napoleon Bonaparte

Désirée (1954)
Henry Koster

"I know what's ahead. I'm one of the men who make history."
—Napoleon Bonaparte

It's a peculiarity of Hollywood films to approach the monumental character of Napoleon only through his illicit affairs. There's nothing about his glories—the Italian and Egyptian campaigns, Austerlitz—or his fall—the collapse at Waterloo or the desolate solitude of Saint Helena. And, if we must be interested in his private life, there's still nothing about his great love, Josephine de Beauharnais, the proud beauty of the islands, the disowned Empress of Malmaison, nor about Marie Louise of Austria, his wife of convenience, the mother of the King of Rome. Beginning in 1937, however, an obscure Polish mistress, Countess Maria Walewska, enjoyed the recognition of MGM, who lent her Greta Garbo's noble looks. Then, in 1954, the hour of glory arrived for Bonaparte's very first fiancée, Désirée Clary, the Marseille merchant's daughter whose path led indeed to a fabulous destiny.[71] More than the romance with Marie Walewska, this story is irresistible—the young commoner has nothing but her beauty until her meeting with an unknown Bonaparte changes everything dramatically and leads her, through a series of events, to finish her life on the Swedish throne. Already you can see the screenwriters rubbing their hands: why wear yourself out thinking up a fairy tale when real life gives you one ready-made? However, Désirée would not wed her prince, the somber Corsican general she loved before Europe even knew the name of Bonaparte. She married Jean-Baptiste Bernadotte, an important figure in the Grande Armée who would come to turn against the Emperor—in a spectacular dramatic twist—thus providing a perfect counterpoint to his excesses. This is the likely explanation for Hollywood's skipping over some of his exploits: Napoleon is a great man without being a hero. And in the United States of the 1950s, his appetite for conquest dangerously recalled that of the Soviet enemy. There isn't a period film from this era that didn't slightly distort history in the hope to extract some measure of anticommunism.

The Crucial Choice of a Napoleon

Of course, the title and the pretty face of Jean Simmons promise a beautiful heroine, a spirited and romantic female figure. Yet Twentieth Century Fox was well aware that the success of *Désirée*'s casting depended wholly on the choice of its Napoleon. They contacted Montgomery Clift, who refused, as the role seemed too much of a stretch to him; without much conviction, they looked at Louis Jourdan and a few other Hollywood Frenchmen. It so happened that Henry Koster, the director, a Napoleon book buff, had learned from reading Stendhal that the young Bonaparte "was classically cut; he was a man of Plutarch."[72] Wasn't there a young actor out there with a noble profile, the realest Roman tribune of them all? In the end, who could play the "greatest man to have appeared in the world since Caesar"[73] better than Mark Antony? Marlon Brando thus inherited the role without ever knowing whether he truly wanted it. You can't refuse Napoleon, he told himself, half reassured about his acting ability by *On the Waterfront*, its awards and success. But quite quickly he confided to the film's producer, Julian Blaustein, that he felt "scared to death that he was going to look like 'all the lunatics in the various institutions' around the country who think they're Napoleon."[74] For the first time in his career, Brando had to confront not a role but a myth, an icon that audiences had a preconceived image of. And as much as he swore no one would catch him slipping his hand in his vest, as the traditional iconography seemed to impose, he spent hours in front of a mirror reworking his face with his personal makeup artist, Philip Rhodes. The fake nose worked fairly well, though he needed a curlier forelock, slightly blacker eyes, a less generous lip: the face of Jacques Louis David's Napoleon was within reach, but something was always keeping them from reproducing it exactly. Luckily, there was the personality! There, no doubt, Brando had real points in common with his character. Like the Emperor, he was conscious of having a destiny and had no scruples about recruiting any passerby to fulfill it. There was just one difference: our young star showed a terrible lack of imperial gravitas. One day, Henry Koster found him sitting

Marlon Brando on the set of Henry Koster's *Désirée* (1954).

behind a set piece fountain. Everyone was waiting
for him to start the shoot, but Brando remained
silent, his gaze fixed on the fountain. Finally,
he revealed what was bothering him: "I wish this
fountain was full of chocolate ice-cream soda.
[…] Because I like chocolate ice-cream sodas!"
The day of the coronation scene, Brando
organized a squirt gun fight that got out of hand.
It took several hours for the extras, sprayed
by the studio's fire hoses, to be ready again for
filming. A single warning shot from the producer
— shocked by such silliness — reestablished order
on the set. Unfortunately, Henry Koster wielded
no such authority. As soon as he gave some
direction to his Napoleon, he'd consistently get
sent packing, to the point that he soon ceased
to make the slightest suggestion.

A Destiny Stronger Than Love

This made way, then, without a director's filter,
for Marlon Brando's Napoleon. Despite a few
French "mademoiselles" in the script that he
punctuates his lines with, his accent goes back
and forth strangely between His Majesty's
English and that of Brando's Nebraskan fore-
bears. Apart from that, he is loyal to the legend:
as haughty and touchy as you like, with a solemn
air and brusque manners. *Désirée*, to say the
least, doesn't pretend to be realistic. The Clarys'
Marseille salon looks like what it is — a stage

setting. Yet from the entrance of Napoleone —
as the young Corsican was still called — the artifice
of this setup ceases to get in the way. Not because
Brando is a realistic Bonaparte, but, whereas Jean
Simmons, in all the youthfulness of her twenty-
five years, plays her role with naïve spontaneity,
he has the intelligence to integrate the inevitable
theatricality of the film into his performance.
As if aware of the uniqueness of this role, Brando
dispenses with his usual attributes — quick,
unexpected movements, gestures of touching his
face with his hand, inaudible mumblings. Here,
he speaks clearly, in a lower tone than normal,
maintaining a measured delivery close to that
of *Julius Caesar*. As soon as he appears at the
Clarys' — with his brother Joseph, at Désirée's
invitation — it's like a page out of Stendhal:
"Napoleon, at twenty-one or twenty-two, must
have been quite different from what one in Paris
called a nice young man. […] He had a strong
mind; he had the strictest logic. He had read
extensively […]. His mind was sharp and quick,
his speech energetic."[75] It's true that at the Clarys',
Napoleone conducts what should be pleasant
socializing as if it were a military meeting (just as
he will a bit later scold — reversing their roles — a
soldier who's come to arrest him after Robespierre's
death). "And now which one of you two ladies
would be kind enough to show me your garden?"
he asks the Clary sisters in a neutral tone, without
the least hint of flirting. "Women liked him for

his new and proud ideas, for his bold arguments,"[76] Stendhal tells us. In fact, the evening stroll of Désirée and General Bonaparte is, thanks to Brando, a most original scene of seduction. In a semidarkness so overworked it has the effect of day for night, the young woman listens, fascinated, as the unknown general rolls out his dreams of greatness. When he asks her when the marriage of Joseph Bonaparte and Julie Clary will be celebrated, Désirée protests, "But last night they had not even met!" "Last night you and I had not even met," replies Napoleon without flinching. Not for an instant does Brando let himself play the smooth talker: his mouth smiles but his eyes remain grave, and despite his clear desire for his pretty companion, love always seems the least of his concerns. The result is that what should be, given the dialogue, a totally conventional romantic scene becomes a scene of action. Napoleon grabs Désirée's arm, and it's a military victory that takes shape: "I would probably kiss you before very long." Ah, yes indeed, they must get to the kiss, the inevitable climax of every Hollywood romance, but to make it happen, Napoleon skips the compliments and other promises of eternal love. He prefers to give a lecture about "La Marseillaise," which will soon ring out across Europe, and to announce, staring off into the distance, "I know what's ahead. I'm one of the men who make history." The line's a tough one. How do you get people to believe

in the supernatural foresight of a Bonaparte who has yet to distinguish himself and, with a grandiose tone, in the context of a lover's tryst? Happily for him, Brando remembered what he'd learned from Kazan: how to suggest the opposite of what's said in the dialogue, instead of mimicking its contents. So his Napoleon's megalomaniacal proclamations are uttered in a soft voice, without grandiloquence. And then, sure of himself without ever being arrogant, he approaches the young woman slowly and, his gaze riveted on her lips, finally kisses her.

The first part of the film is carried along by the energy of this youthful love that has Napoleon pursuing the young Mademoiselle Clary while she chooses silks in the family store, perched high up on a ladder, or turning up in the dead of night to kiss her passionately with disregard for bourgeois propriety. Nevertheless, it's difficult for the viewer to embrace the cause of the young Bonaparte. Like Désirée, always vaguely uneasy in his presence, we are wary of this soldier with his dark looks and rough manners. Brando succeeds here in using to his character's benefit a distinctive feature of his face that turns out to be clearly more problematic in *Guys and Dolls* (Joseph L. Mankiewicz, 1955): the odd combination of a would-be winning smile and an expression of infinite sadness. The trait is striking in the scene where Napoleon comes to bid Désirée farewell on the doorstep of her home the night of a terrible storm. While a driving rain pelts the two love-birds, Bonaparte asks Désirée's brother, who, troubled by a noise, has opened his window, for the young woman's hand. It might be the most unromantic marriage proposal in the history of Hollywood cinema: no profound look of love or passionate embrace, but a healthy dose of anger in his voice and an extremely stern face. Brushing aside the sarcastic refusal of Monsieur Clary — "One Bonaparte is quite enough in a family" — Napoleon turns back to Désirée and makes the same proposal without further ceremony. "Yes. Oh, yes!" she exclaims, which inspires a smile from her intended, worrisome in that it lacks real joy. In other words, when Napoleon heads off toward Paris shouting to his ladylove to remember he adores her, we know perfectly well there's a strong chance he won't keep his promise.

In short, Marlon Brando's choices at the start of *Désirée* are far from obvious. He is so solemn, so little interested in matters of love that we struggle to understand why the carefree Désirée feels such a lifelong passion for him. And his uneasy smiles at moments let us believe he's hiding beneath his harmless exterior the urges of a psychopath. We must wait until the end of their brief love affair for this performance to make more sense. Désirée, having had no news of her intended since the notorious night of the storm, heads to Paris, where she's heard Napoleon is living the high life. She hopes to get an explanation or perhaps reconciliation. She slips into Madame Tallien's elegant salon, thanks to the help of Bernadotte (Michael Rennie), and she catches sight of Napoleon lying back innocently against a flamboyant femme fatale, Josephine de Beauharnais (Merle Oberon). In the shot, where he doesn't know Désirée is watching him, the actor shows absolute detachment, as if his mind were some-where else. But suddenly, he sees her, surges to his feet and cries out in his soft voice, "Désirée!" It's one of the rare moments of the film where Brando seems to believe in this love story and puts a little fire in it. Désirée throws her glass in Josephine's face, and Napoleon, frowning, backs away as though afraid. What a beautiful romantic movie this could've been! On the one hand, a Désirée who is naïve and childlike, yes, but also zesty, surprising, full of nerve; on the other hand, a Bonaparte who is solemn, of course, but also human, sensitive, certainly more in love than he himself knows. Alas, this chemistry is but fleeting and will not be reproduced in more than a few other instances. The rest of the time, Jean Simmons and Brando seem to be, even despite themselves, in different films, she waiting for some romanticism from him that never comes, and he oblivious to her the more he obsesses over his own greatness. We are far from the subtlety of Charles Broyer,

who, in *Conquest*, manages to make us experience the shift from Bonaparte the revolutionary to the power-hungry Emperor.

Brando Shines as an Authoritarian Emperor

Where Brando does excel, on the other hand, is in the vitriolic portrait of an authoritarian Napoleon who seems to have as his sole adversary Désirée's husband, the rather colorless Bernadotte. After becoming Emperor, when Napoleon learns that Bernadotte, not satisfied with accepting the throne of Sweden, wishes to renounce his French nationality, Brando offers up a memorable scene of anger: "Will you remind him that he's a Frenchman? And that his Emperor has a right to command him!" He shouts, he raves, his chair falls over, and when he signs the order, it's with still visible rage. So much exaggeration has the effect of a caricature, that of an authoritarian power the film itself rejects, preferring Bernadotte's clear moderation. But let's go back a bit. When she sees the First Consul for the first time after their very public breakup, Désirée is still furious: "I should like to throw these candlesticks at you." Napoleon retains an Olympian calm: "Well, if you must, at least don't set fire to the place," he replies, extinguishing each flame with his fingers, an on-the-set improvisation of Brando's that gives the character a tinge of true grandeur. Indifferent to pain and even to female jealously, does this Napoleon have any weakness? But his best moment comes later on, during the coronation rehearsal. With one hand behind his back and the other in his vest, Napoleon watches his sisters and the ladies of the court as they rehearse the procession. His expression is that of a great organizer, a director satisfied with his creatures. Suddenly, the three sisters let go of Josephine's train: the role of simple followers seems beneath them; they would like to be princesses at the very least. It's then that Napoleon grows angry, sharpening his voice, that soft, whispered voice that foreshadows *The Godfather* and that he's had since the beginning of the film. Changing his mind suddenly, he orders them to kneel and, sardonically, gives them a tap on the head. "Now each of you is an Imperial Highness. A princess. Now will you kindly rise and carry the train?" Brando's nonchalance, the speed with which he goes from fury to this parody of ennoblement, speaks volume about the incredible arbitrariness of power, the madness of a regime that grants all rights to one man. Likewise, when there's concern about not being able to find the young virgins who must attend the coronation, the future Emperor retorts, "Gentlemen, it is your problem. I'm sure there are at least twelve suitable young ladies left in France." There's a cynicism here that resolutely breaks from Napoleonic legend and gives the character a darker stripe, far from the girlie love affair at the beginning of the film.

Left: Albert Dieudonné in Abel Gance's *Napoléon* (1927).

Right: Herbert Lom in King Vidor's *War and Peace* (1956).

Napoleon Bonaparte—consul or emperor, general or prisoner, lover or father, military genius or tyrant—has enjoyed incredibly good cinematic fortune since the early days of film. Napoleon is pictured in all of his complexities, from Abel Gance's and Sacha Guitry's majestic portraits of him to the caricatures sketched by Woody Allen or Terry Gilliam.

Albert Dieudonné in *Napoléon* (Abel Gance, 1927)

Paul Muni, who is disturbing in *Seven Faces* (Berthold Viertel, 1929)

Charles Boyer in *Conquest* (Clarence Brown, 1937)

Jean-Louis Barrault in *Le Destin fabuleux de Désirée Clary* (Sacha Guitry, 1942)

Herbert Lom in *War and Peace* (King Vidor, 1956)

Dennis Hopper in *The Story of Mankind* (Irwin Allen, 1957)

Rod Steiger in *Waterloo* (Sergei Bondarchuk, 1970)

James Tolkan in *Love and Death* (Woody Allen, 1975)

Ian Holm in *Time Bandits* (Terry Gilliam, 1981)

Patrice Chéreau in *Adieu Bonaparte* (Youssef Chahine, 1985)

Alain Chabat in *Night at the Museum: Battle of the Smithsonian* (Shawn Levy, 2009)

The day of the coronation, this will to control is brought to light: Napoleon, with a darker expression than ever, takes the crown from Pope Pius VII's hands. And without paying any attention to the crowd's astonishment, he crowns himself. Here we're at a critical moment of the legend where Brando succeeds not only in truly resembling the well-known pictures of the Emperor but also in recreating something of his personality. To take the crown from the Pope and to set it on his own head, he employs an extremely theatrical gesture. It's one of these melodramatic moments where the actor seems to underscore the fact that he's at the height of his performance. For what is this moment of Napoleon's gesture if not stagecraft, a political message, a way to tell the world that Napoleon I will submit to no authority, neither human nor even divine? Only Désirée defies his implacable law: the day of the coronation, she does not appear in sky blue as demanded earlier by His Majesty, but rather in beautiful flamboyant red, a sign of disobedience that, as frivolous as it may be, is no less admirable, and which attracts, we suspect, the umpteenth disapproving look from the new Emperor.

A More Complex Character Emerges

Due to its luxurious costumes and the prestige of its actors, *Désirée* has the look of an epic film, while at heart it's an intimate portrait, without a battle scene or even a political meeting. In the first part, Bonaparte's triumphs are shown through a few close-ups of objects—a vase, a painting, a medallion bearing his likeness. Nor will much of the Empire's story be told, except for the divorce from Josephine and Napoleon's quarrels with Bernadotte, which serve as a symbol of the confrontation between ambition and reason, dictatorship and good government. The repudiation of Josephine leads to a public ceremony, during which the Empress collapses while the Emperor remains unperturbed. That evening, Désirée, having come to the palace to console Josephine, stumbles upon Napoleon in a small sitting room plunged in darkness that she's tried to cross through as quietly as possible, in bare feet. In any case, Brando promptly grabs Jean Simmons's shoes and in doing so obliges her to stay with him. "Citizen Désirée," he murmurs nostalgically, gazing at her. And, as always when Napoleon is in a romantic mood, he gives an order: "Teach me [to waltz]." It hardly matters if his companion protests. "Here. And now," he proclaims, taking it upon himself to embrace her. He barely accepts that she refuses him a kiss. "I will not try to kiss you again. Let us waltz." In its very strangeness, the scene is beautiful, establishing for the first time since Madame Tallien's salon a real involvement

between the film's protagonists. As during their walk through the Clarys' garden, Brando makes it clear that, for his Napoleon, military command and amorous desire are one and the same. Much later in the film, another sequence picks up on this idea. Distressed by the Russian campaign, Napoleon visits Désirée in the middle of the night to ask for her help—Bernadotte, now King of Sweden, must stop aiding the Russians. The scene contains an obvious erotic ambiguity: Désirée, who didn't expect the visit, goes down to the salon in her nightgown. "Did you obtain that dress in Sweden?" the Emperor tenderly asks his former fiancée, who's become a queen despite herself. "It looks good on you." Since this is the first time in the film that he's played a vulnerable man, Brando finds inspiration in his best performances. He uses all the set dressings, warms his hands on the meager flame of a candle—as if the Russian winter still chilled him to the bone—caresses a small box he once gave to Désirée, and finally confesses: "I have come from the steppes of Russia, where my soldiers lie buried. The ones that still live are snow-blind, and they whimper and cry like children." In this moment, Brando makes a strange, unexpected gesture, one that doesn't appear in any of his other films. For a long moment, he places his index fingers in the corners of his eyes. Suddenly, his Napoleon seems filled with the pain of the Grande Armée, to the point of feeling it physically. Here he is laid low by the suffering of his soldiers, at the mercy of a woman who could decide to write to her husband or not. "That is why you came to see me," Désirée realizes, vaguely disappointed. "Yes," Napoleon admits. Then after a beat: "And because I was… cold and tired and alone."

Thus, little by little, thanks to the performance Brando constructed and that Henry Koster was forced to agree to, there emerges a Napoleon who is more complex than he first appears. A hot-tempered, absolute monarch who desires power for himself and his family, and who crushes anyone who gets in his way. But also a good general who loves his troops, a lover who remains faithful, at least in spirit—Désirée remains his one true love throughout the film—and finally, a father. In a short scene of a reception at the imperial palace, we see him carry his baby in his arms: a moment of tenderness, and the one and only time in the film when Brando smiles with his whole being and suggests true joy. The final scene, the last meeting between the two great lovers, brings together all of these aspects. More than ever the artifice is visible: Brando and Jean Simmons talk in front of a painted backcloth that features a beautiful summer sky. Napoleon has been defeated and must surrender himself to the English. Désirée is sent to try to convince him to give himself up or else "the city will be destroyed." As he is about to relinquish his ephemeral but intoxicating earthly glory, the Emperor reflects

The last meeting of the two
great lovers: Désirée attempts
to convince the defeated
Napoleon to give himself up.

on his life and his failures: "I dreamt of United States of Europe. […] One law, one coin, and one people." The script has never suggested, before this line, such a noble design, but never mind: Brando recovers his confidence, his intensity from the very first scenes, and, once again the ardent general from the film's beginning, he makes us believe in a Europe at peace under his aegis. When he hands his sword to Désirée as a sign of his surrender, he ventures an affectionate reprimand: "Please don't hold it like an umbrella." With this note of amused tenderness and uncommon detachment, while the legend's gravest moment plays out, Brando brings a subtle nuance that lightens the melodrama, like a compelling final touch to the portrait of one legend by another.

5

Rio

One-Eyed Jacks (1961)
Marlon Brando

"You may be a one-eyed jack around here, but I've seen the other side of your face."
—Rio

He had everyone worried! The magnificent, temperamental, megalomaniacal Brando was going to direct a film and act in it, too. Who did he think he was, Orson Welles? Or worse, Charlie Chaplin, as the great Truman Capote wrote with discreet irony in his 1957 *New Yorker* profile on the star.[77] How could Marlon, the first-time filmmaker, possibly know how to direct Brando, the world's best actor? Would the unpredictable egomaniac succeed in transforming into a rigorous, demanding director, capable of leading a crew, of yielding to the needs of everyone, of keeping to a budget? Those with enough faith in his genius to believe in this crazy project were no less afraid. The chance Brando had dreamed of, this unique opportunity to show everyone what he was capable of, might very well end with him shooting himself in the foot. Suppose, for example, he let himself get carried away, that the actor in him hijacked the film in the service of his pervasive narcissism… Could there be better proof that, despite his genius, Brando was mostly unemployable?

Brando: Actor, Director, Producer

The film *One-Eyed Jacks* is first and foremost a game for all or nothing, the risk—taken in full awareness by the greatest star in the world—of destroying his own career, and in one fell swoop, too. Brando's desire to direct was pressing, impossible to silence, and due largely to his staggering, overwhelming, and, in the film, oh-so-striking attraction to self-destruction. In 1955, shortly after winning the Oscar for Best Actor for *On the Waterfront*, the actor announced that he had launched his own production company, Pennebaker, Inc.,[78] in association with his father and George Englund. There was undoubtedly a genuine financial concern here, a convenient means of better managing his income. And, even more important, there was a desire for control: as producer of the films he starred in, Brando would ensure his choice of directors—and thus prevent the misfortune he experienced with Henry Koster, the director of *Désirée* (1954), who had

too quickly abdicated any ambition to direct him, or Joshua Logan, the creator of *Sayonara* (1957), who was, to the contrary, stubborn when they clashed.

Like Kirk Douglas or Burt Lancaster before him, Marlon Brando the producer looked for subjects that might be suitable for Marlon Brando the actor. He caused a stir by announcing his intention to make a pro-Indian film and engage a screenwriter to adapt a novel about a bunch of cattle ranchers out West. The message was clear: Brando was dying to make a Western. Was it nostalgia for the great West where he was born? The sign of a deeper aspiration to become a true American myth? The land of Westerns is, of course, one of legends, a fertile land of nation-forging myths. And it was indeed a Western screenplay Brando got excited about—even if there were no Indians or cattle ranchers to speak of. In April 1958, Pennebaker, Inc., bought the adaptation of Charles Neider's novel *The Authentic Death of Hendry Jones*, written by a virtual unknown, Sam Peckinpah, a television scriptwriter at the time. Taken with the script, Brando nevertheless undertook to change it from start to finish. He hired Stanley Kubrick—recently hailed for *Paths of Glory* (1957)—to rewrite it and, dissatisfied with the work of the future director of *The Wild Bunch* (1969), he unceremoniously fired Peckinpah… So the summer of 1958 saw Brando and Kubrick working one-on-one in his mansion on Mulholland Drive. Of these sessions amid the stuffy heat of a Californian summer, all we know is that the atmosphere was peculiar to say the least: Kubrick at the typewriter, bare-chested and in his underwear, Brando banging a monumental gong whenever he wanted to impose his point of view, all of it punctuated with a few memorable arguments.

Yes, the gong surely sounded frequently, for there was no lack of disagreement between the two legends. Should Dad Longworth be played by Spencer Tracy—as Kubrick wished, since he put a lot of stock in casting against type—or by Karl Malden, Brando's old acting partner from the Kazan years, a true friend whom he adored? Should the saga of Rio, Brando's role, end tragically or offer the character and his sweetheart a final shot at happiness? In the end, depending on the version, Kubrick either quit the film or was

Marlon Brando on the set of his first film as a director, *One-Eyed Jacks* (1961).

77

fired. In a *Playboy* interview, Brando summed
up the facts with a good dose of bad faith: "Just
before we were to start, Stanley said, 'Marlon,
I don't know what the picture's about.' I said, 'I'll
tell you what it's about. It's about $300,000 that
I've already paid Karl Malden.' He said, 'Well,
if that's what it's about, I'm in the wrong picture.'
So that was the end of it. I ran around, asked
Sidney Lumet, Gadg, and, I don't know, four or
five people, nobody wanted to direct it. There
wasn't anything for me to do except to direct it or
go to the poorhouse."[79] Though hardly believable,
the explanation allowed Brando to avoid revealing
how much he had invested in this film, which
from the beginning was his own project.

The Two Faces of Rio

The title *One-Eyed Jacks* points to the opposing
pair of the jack of spades and the jack of hearts
and in the film refers to the two mortal enemies
Rio and Longworth. Nicknamed Dad, Longworth
is clearly a father figure for Rio a.k.a. "The Kid",
his student in banditry and his boundless admirer.
The inseparable outlaw duo splits up as the film
opens when, fleeing a holdup gone wrong, Dad
chooses to save his own skin, deliberately letting
his accomplice get caught by the Mexicans.
The story of the film will be one of vengeance—
meticulously planned by Rio over the course
of his five years in prison—executed with care

and marked, of course, by a few fateful errors
along the way. For during his partner's imprisonment, Dad has turned over a new leaf. When Rio
finds him again, he's leading a respectable life
as a small-town sheriff, with a haughty wife and
a young stepdaughter. What better revenge for
Rio than to dishonor that stepdaughter, the pure,
innocent, sweet Louisa? The plan has one flaw:
it doesn't take into account the possibility of love
and the deep attachment that Rio will come to
feel toward the girl.

In the press pack that accompanied the film's
release in 1961, Brando speaks of his character
in these terms: "Our early-day heroes were not
brave one hundred percent of the time, nor were
they good one hundred percent of the time.
My part is that of a man who is intuitive and
suspicious, prideful and searching. He has a touch
of the vain and a childish and disproportionate
sense of virtue and manly ethics. He is lonely and
generally distrustful of human contacts."[80] This
statement is so true that the word "heroes" seems
completely out of place. Rio is not a hero, but
rather a complex character, a sinner miraculously
redeemed by love. At the beginning of the film,
he manages to get a kiss from a girl after giving
her a ring stolen from another woman: "My
mother gave me this ring just before she died,"
he lies to her with a sly smile and a smoldering
look. At the end, the same Rio appears serious, his
eyes somber, promising eternal love to Louisa.

In November 1957, Truman Capote wrote a profile of Marlon Brando in the *New Yorker*, "The Duke in His Domain," which sparked the anger of its subject—who was furious that the novelist and journalist should have published his confidential remarks—and which even today remains one of the finest pieces written about the star.

Extract: "When he speaks of the boy he was, the boy seems to inhabit him, as if time had done little to separate the man from the hurt, desiring child. […] 'But my mother was everything to me. A whole world. I tried so hard. I used to come home from school…' He hesitated, as though waiting for me to picture him: Bud, books under his arm, scuffling his way along an afternoon street. 'There wouldn't be anybody home. Nothing in the icebox.' More lantern slides: empty rooms, a kitchen. 'Then the telephone would ring. Somebody calling from some bar. And they'd say, "We've got a lady down here. You better come get her."' Suddenly, Brando was silent. In silence the picture faded, or, rather, became fixed: Bud at the telephone. At last, the image moved again, leaped forward in time. Bud is eighteen, and: 'I thought if she loved me enough, trusted me enough, I thought, then we can be together, in New York; we'll live together and I'll take care of her. Once, later on, that really happened. She left my father and came to live with me. In New York, when I was in a play. I tried so hard. But my love wasn't enough. […] And one day'— the flatness of his voice grew flatter, yet the emotional pitch ascended until one could discern like a sound within a sound, a wounded bewilderment—'I didn't care any more. She was there. In a room. Holding on to me. And I let her fall. Because I couldn't take it any more— watch her breaking apart, in front of me, like a piece of porcelain. I stepped right over her. I walked right out. I was indifferent. Since then, I've been indifferent.'"

In fact, the film follows his journey toward honesty, a journey that's also a veritable Way of the Cross. And the two jacks, the two faces of the title, are the two sides of Rio himself, the tormentor and the victim. Quite a *tour de force*, since Brando allows these two aspects of Rio to coexist in his performance without them ever taking away from each other. In other words, the sincere Rio at the end of the film doesn't let us forget for one second the cynic of the beginning. That would be too simple. If he is neither "consistently brave" nor "consistently good," Rio is most certainly a two-sided man.

The Director at Work

When it came to directing his costars, Brando the filmmaker resorted to a strategy identical in every way to Brando the actor's: intimidation and undermining. Larry Duran, a Marine veteran Marlon became infatuated with and whom he placed in small roles beginning with *Viva Zapata!* (1952), wasn't always comfortable in the most demanding scenes. To make him react, Brando quite simply hit him. Similarly, he fired some gunshots in the air to provoke a reaction from Pina Pellicer, the Mexican actress who landed the role of Louisa. Hoping to get around the young woman's anxiety, at its height each time the camera rolled, he discreetly asked his director of photography, Charles Lang, to film what Pina

thought was a mere rehearsal of the difficult scene in which she admits to her mother that she's pregnant. His clashes with Karl Malden were also lively: Brando spits in his partner's face in the scene where Dad whips Rio and thus earns his most authentic indignation. Yet their friendship came out even stronger from this test. In an interview with Peter Manso, Malden confided: "I trusted his eyes."[81] A nice declaration of faith that speaks to how much Brando was, deep down, a director.

Incidentally, Brando the actor did everything he could to enhance the skills of his acting partners. With extreme equanimity, he made a radical performance choice that he would use again in *Mutiny on the Bounty* (1962). Was it a sign of his absolute, and perhaps exaggerated, confidence in his own magnetism? The influence of a book on Zen he gave to his circle of friends at the time? Or was it because he knew well, as an experienced star, that the viewer's eyes would remain fixed on him even if he deliberately chose to do the least possible? This was a way, by contrast, to make Karl Malden's dramatic range stand out and to favor the interests of the film over his own. The scene of their reunion—which marks, five years after Dad Longworth's fateful desertion, the beginning of Rio's revenge—is an example of this. Dad is lying on the veranda of his secluded house near the ocean. In front of him, the bars of the railing that frame his face seem

already to carry out the punishment Rio has in mind for him, imprisonment. In a reverse angle shot, a triumphant Rio approaches on his horse. Brando allows the tension to linger, savoring the contrast between the horizontal and the vertical, between the obvious poise of one body and the immobility of the other.

Finally, Rio finds himself facing Dad. The shot–reverse shot is taken from a slightly low angle with the blue sky in the background. Never will the film make more clear how alike the two mortal enemies are: they are filmed, and framed, in the same way. Their behavior is identical—both lie through their teeth, Rio swearing to Dad that nothing's happened to him since Dad's desertion, Dad professing an everlasting friendship for his old partner. But Malden is all smiles and raised eyebrows; his voice takes on a thousand different inflections; he is the picture of exuberance. Brando, on the other hand, holds himself back, remaining serious, with a fixed gaze. If he touches his face, it's an event: for no gesture, even the slightest, escapes him inadvertently. A bit later, during a second confrontation—at the small local fiesta that will allow Rio to seduce Dad's stepdaughter—Malden again adds to the feigned camaraderie with a series of roaring laughs. He acts deliberately fake. Much like Brando, who embodies absolute control emphatically and seems to calculate even the slightest flicker of his eyelid. This is when the almost Pirandellian dimension of the film emerges: both of them are putting on an act, in the true sense of the word. That is to say, together they flaunt the fact that they're actors and that they're performing a piece written in advance. And this corresponds entirely with Brando's view of his profession: "Everybody is an actor, you spend your whole day acting. Everybody has suffered through moments where you're thinking one thing and feeling one thing and not showing it. That's acting. […] Acting is just hustling. Some people are hustling money, some power."[82] Others still, like Rio, to take revenge on their mortal enemy.

This whole setup collapses when the situation is reversed and Dad takes his own revenge on Rio in a scene that has been the subject of much discussion. The sheriff takes his former partner in crime out to the public square, rips the back of Rio's shirt, and gives him a long whipping. Instead of falling down under these lashes as we would expect, Brando slowly lowers himself as if broken by the whip. He hardly cries out. No close up, but a distant, almost neutral view of the wounds cutting into his flesh. The torture doesn't stop there: Dad breaks his victim's right hand and then perches him on a horse like a puppet with its strings cut. This nicely mirrors their first big confrontation, when Rio approached Dad on his horse and Dad was trapped behind his railing. Like before, Rio is on his horse, Dad below him, only now Rio, who seemed to dominate the earlier

situation, is bleeding and presses his broken hand to his chest. From then on, the shift in the actors' performance is obvious. Malden becomes more restrained. In his grimacing smiles from the first part, we have to discern the savagery that, given free rein in this scene of great violence, finally subsides. Brando, to the contrary, is more expressive; he dares unexpected and audacious poses—like the reclining nude one he strikes when Louise comes to find him on the beach where he's recovering from his wounds. In another scene, he throws an angry fit, sends a table flying, and shows us there's still a Stanley Kowalski lying dormant inside him.

An Autobiographical Role?

With the help of Charles Lang, his remarkable director of photography, Brando the director certainly adapted to this change of atmosphere: he filmed himself for the first time in a close-up, under extremely elaborate lighting that emphasized his eyes. The affection Brando the director feels for Brando the character does not become apparent until his Way of the Cross. If the first half of the film is about self-hatred—with a ruthless Brando at its center who uses his acting talent to torture innocent women—the second half is one of empathy for a man who suffers. In a scene that evokes The Mocking of Christ paintings of the Italian Renaissance, Rio is brought back to town in handcuffs. Manhandled by the mob, he finds himself once again behind bars, humiliated and powerless. This is when the critical question is raised that lies at the heart of the film for Brando fans: Is Rio a self-portrait? Must we see this peculiar film as the decisive moment when Marlon Brando reveals to us his vision of himself? Remember the worried buzz that surrounded the shooting. For if people in the actor's circle were concerned about this venture, it was because they sensed, beyond the inconsequential costs or the typical hazards of making a film, the risk he took in revealing his profound masochism to the world.

This masochism, or at least a certain liking for self-destruction, showed even in Brando's personal life during the shoot. Katy Jurado, who played Dad's wife, was one of his longtime mistresses. He began no less than a parallel affair with Pina Pellicer, the actress playing Louisa, whom he crudely nick-named "Pigeon" and mistreated despite her obvious psychological frailty.[83] The star also suffered dreadful attacks of bulimia that forced costume designer Yvonne Wood to sew him eighteen identical pairs of pants in different sizes. On set, he displayed boundless generosity, for example, paying for the hundred or so crew members' Christmas vacation, but he could also be unbearable, once waiting for hours on end for the perfect wave to have in the background of the big love scene with Louisa. In short, the inner turmoil of the actor–director was felt on the set, and in the film.

The scene in which Dad gives Rio a whipping inspired Quentin Tarantino for his film Reservoir Dogs.

"The personification of the Brando mystique and one of the greatest [directorial] debuts of all time"[b] is how Quentin Tarantino matter-of-factly sums up *One-Eyed Jacks*, a film he readily cites as among his ten favorites in the history of cinema. Indeed, it's hardly surprising that the maker of *Kill Bill* (2003)—whose taste for blood is no secret—revels in a film where Karl Malden slashes Marlon Brando's back with a whip. The scene in question contains a metaphor of the director's powerlessness—Brando, as star and director, submits to the blows of his actor and character—which was incidentally taken up in similar fashion in *Reservoir Dogs* (1992): when Mr. Blonde (Michael Madsen) listens to music while cutting off the ear of a policeman bound to a chair, it's the filmmaker himself who seems to get a kick out of the torture he can inflict on his inevitably silent and immobilized audience.

Rio attempts to fight off his jailers.

Opposite: A grueling shoot that lasted more than six months.

So, why all the distress? We don't have to look far to recognize in the destructive link that binds Dad and Rio a variation on the relationship between Marlon and his father. In *Last Tango in Paris*, when invited by Bertolucci to improvise a monologue about his childhood, Brando recounted the humiliation he felt as a teenager when his father made him milk a cow before a date with a girl. The memory was still so searing that it came to the actor spontaneously as soon as he was asked to share a piece of his private life. The same thing happens during a moment in *One-Eyed Jacks* that one could describe, like Bertolucci did his own film, as "a psychoanalytic adventure."[84] "I've seen the other side of your face," Rio says to Dad when he finds himself behind bars the second time thanks to his spiritual father. It's a moment of truth where the revered mentor reveals his hostility and the promise of happiness goes sour. In this sense, *One-Eyed Jacks* is no surprise to a loyal Brando fan: who could've believed his outlook was happy or optimistic when his melancholic face had darkened the bubbliest of musical comedies (*Guys and Dolls*, 1955) and the world of the greatest comic of all time, Charlie Chaplin (*A Countess from Hong Kong*, 1967)? If childhood scars and innate sadness explain the film's tone, Brando's contempt for his profession must also be taken into account. At the start of the shoot, he told *The Los Angeles Times*, "I have no respect for acting. Acting by

and large is the expression of a neurotic impulse. I've never in my life met an actor who was not neurotic. […] Acting is a bum's life, in that it leads to perfect self-indulgence. […] Quitting acting—that is the mark of maturity."[85] Is this nothing but provocation, false cynicism? Perhaps. But it must be noted that over time, his talk remains exactly the same. Thirty years later, we hear the same refrain: "I don't think any movie is a work of art. I simply do not."[86]

According to this logic, the whole association the first part established between lying and acting seems to be a narrative strategy to arrive at the character's carefully orchestrated punishment. Because he manipulates everyone he meets, because he feigns emotions that he doesn't feel, Rio will suffer a long involved punishment. *One-Eyed Jacks* is the story of a man who pays for his lies and therefore his taste for acting, as illustrated by the notorious ring that Rio steals and then claims is a gift from his deceased mother, and later by the necklace he buys at the market and offers to Louisa in their big seduction scene. The logic of the film—following the inner logic of its creator—wants Rio to pay for his talent for swindling, his ability to make people believe his tall tales, in short, his obvious gift for the actor's craft. This severity, this stern moral code that leaves no room for imagination is a direct inheritance from Marlon Senior, who was so opposed to the idea that his only son should

choose a career as an actor. "My father was indifferent to me," Brando confessed to Truman Capote. "Nothing I could do interested him, or pleased him."[87]

A Happy or a Tragic Ending?

The real surprise of the film is that redemption through love should be possible. Possible thanks to the studio's commercial demands — horrified by the darkness of the first cut, the producer demanded a new, more optimistic third act. And possible thanks as well to the honesty Brando shows in his character. The ending the actor–director hoped for was indeed tragic: while dying, Dad killed his stepdaughter in revenge for the dishonor she'd brought on him by carrying the child of his sworn enemy. Since Paramount didn't see things the same way, the story ends, after Dad's death, with a final meeting between the two lovers, who promise to find each other again someday. We'd love to see the original ending, but it must be noted that the scene we know works beautifully, even though it was shot several months after the rest of the film had been finished just to satisfy the studio. This is proof of Brando's success in portraying the improbable couple of Louisa and Rio. Their first love scene by the sea has the lyricism of Kazan. Here we find the same association, inherited from Romanticism, between raging elements and the feeling of love that the filmmaker idealizes in several films, from *East of Eden* to *Splendor in the Grass*. Rio and Louisa's first kiss is passionate, swathed in sublime chiaroscuro, set over a sound track of waves and music. It's followed by a fade to black, the classic ellipses in Hollywood cinema that leave the night to our imagination and take us directly to the small hours. Then, by the light of day, Rio opens his heart to Louisa. He tells her the truth: why he wanted to find her stepfather and why he has seduced her. As if liberated by the innocence of his young heroine, Brando allows himself an honest love scene in which Rio is divested of all of his tricks. He discovers a new life, without his cynicism and his liking for acting. This new man will rarely leave the seaside again, as if the presence of water guaranteed his inner purity. After the punishment inflicted by Dad, Rio goes to recover from his wounds in a fishermen's hut. Louisa, who knows she's pregnant, comes to him, this time in full awareness. This is when she in turn confesses her love for him. The very final meeting between the lovers takes place, inevitably, against the backdrop of the sea. *One-Eyed Jacks* was shot in spectacular locations, superbly photographed by Charles Lang.

Deeply personal, *One-Eyed Jacks* met the fate of many great films mishandled by the Hollywood system. The cut Brando delivered was four and a half hours. This was unacceptable to Paramount, who first allowed him to propose a three-hour version and then took it back and released a two-hour-and-twenty-minute film. Critics recognized the splendor of this "twilight Western," with its dazzling intensity and its romanticism. But it did not bring in money and left Brando sapped of all his energy, sad and disillusioned — in short, in perfect harmony with the Rio of the film. He told *Newsweek*: "*One-Eyed Jacks* is a potboiler. I think it is quite conventional. It's like spending two years building a chicken coop. When you're finished you want to feel you've done something with your time. It is not an artistic success. I'm a businessman… a captain of industry. Any pretension I've sometimes had of being artistic is now just a long, chilly hope. […] The cinema is not art" It's hard not to see, beneath the ostentatious cynicism, an unhealed wound. Especially when Karl Malden revealed the dedication his director and friend left for him on a production shot: "In remembrance of things that will never be past. We had the very best of each other. That's a lot for our life." It's true that, similar in this regard to that other singular film by a hugely talented actor, *The Night of the Hunter* (Charles Laughton, 1955), *One-Eyed Jacks* — a great and painful film and a sublime self-portrait — will indeed never be past.

6

Fletcher Christian

Mutiny on the Bounty (1962)
Lewis Milestone

"I'm in command of this ship! If there's a man amongst you who doubts that, let me hear his voice."
—Fletcher Christian

Just whisper the title of *Mutiny on the Bounty* and it will conjure up a true legend, that of a mad sixties adventure that delighted the tabloids. Tahiti—its enchanting vistas and smiling wahines—became the setting for an epic shoot that squandered millions from MGM and above all for a love triangle between Brando, an island, and a woman. The romance, glorious in its early years, would later veer toward tragedy. It's heartbreaking in retrospect to read in Lawrence Grobel's book of interviews with Brando the passages concerning the children the actor had with Tarita, the Maimiti of the film. Grobel explains, for example, that Brando "prefers to keep Teihotu and Cheyenne in Tahiti, where they can learn to enjoy life and nature."[88] Marlon Brando apparently believed he had found in Tetiaroa a defense against misfortune. How wrong he was! After the murder of her boyfriend by her half brother Christian, Cheyenne committed suicide at age twenty-five in 1995, leaving her young son orphaned. Whether we view it as just another news item or a classical tragedy, this terrible event inevitably weighs on our perception of *Mutiny on the Bounty*. The story, inspired by a famous historical incident, retraces the mutiny led against the dreaded Captain Bligh (Trevor Howard) by his second in command, Lieutenant Fletcher Christian (Marlon Brando). Sensuality and *joie de vivre* infuse the scenes where Fletcher Christian and his shipmates discover life on the islands where they will live until the end of their days. But to an equal extent, the darkness and self-loathing already present in *One-Eyed Jacks* hangs over the film, as if, beyond the scheduling coincidences that put them back-to-back, the two films were fashioned from the same mold.

A Historical Epic Set Against a Backdrop of Latent Masochism

Like Rio, a character Brando contributed greatly to writing before directing and performing the role, Fletcher Christian is very much a double-sided being, whose greatness emerges only in dramatic reversals and whose unexpected purity is revealed by a love story. Totally unlike the explosive characters Brando played earlier on, such as Stanley Kowalski (*A Streetcar Named Desire*) or even Terry Malloy (*On the Waterfront*), Rio and Christian are introverts, perfectly silent, and mostly impassive. And Brando's approach consists of doing the least possible to transform each gesture, each line of dialogue into an event. The two films also have a common and immediately striking motif: a whipping, inflicted on Brando in *One-Eyed Jacks* and here by various sailors aboard the *Bounty* by order of the fearsome Captain Bligh. In short, the latent masochism of *One-Eyed Jacks* is fully exposed on the *Bounty*, before taking new forms in *Reflections in a Golden Eye* and *Last Tango in Paris*. It's as if *Mutiny on the Bounty*, on paper an entertaining spectacular, became under the influence of its star the portrait of a tormented and complex soul. Not exactly what the producers at MGM had in mind in 1959 when they started working on a new adaptation of the novel by James Norman Hall and Charles Nordhoff in hopes of defeating a powerful and, it seems, invincible enemy: television.

For at the end of the 1950s, more and more audiences were quietly staying at home in front of their small screens instead of treating themselves to a Saturday night movie. This was a problem of scale that forced Hollywood to churn out epics with splendid sets and bold dimensions. The goal? To give viewers their money's worth. *Bounty* belongs to this family of films that run nearly three hours and, like veritable film operas, open with a musical overture. *Spartacus* (Stanley Kubrick, 1960), *Lawrence of Arabia* (David Lean, 1962) and *Cleopatra* (Joseph L. Mankiewicz, 1963), all filmed at about the same time, followed the same rules. The filming of *Bounty* also coincided with the triumph of *Ben-Hur* (William Wyler, 1959), a new adaptation of Lew Wallace's novel previously brought to the screen in 1925 by Fred Niblo. Like that successful historical epic, *Mutiny on the Bounty* had already given rise to a film, directed by Frank Lloyd with Clark Gable and Charles Laughton (1935), a version that took great liberties with the historical reality—notably by adding a happy ending—glowed with

Lieutenant Fletcher Christian, played by Marlon Brando in Lewis Milestone's *Mutiny on the Bounty* (1962).

optimism and energy, and galvanized audiences at the time. Nearly twenty-five years later, the studio, confronted with a crisis of inspiration, decided it was time to revisit the film. They chose the greatest star of the period, Brando, and to give the story a refreshing touch of modernity. For the great novelty of this *Bounty* is that we see the real Tahiti.

Brando Spellbound by Tahiti

And that's exactly what changed everything. For none of the film's producers saw it coming when Marlon Brando fell head over heels for Tahiti. "I always felt an affinity to these islands. Then in 1960, I came down here and it just sort of confirmed what I'd always known,"[89] he declared nearly twenty years later, like a lover soon convinced he was drawn by an irresistible force to his lady. In March 1978, after interminable negotiations, worthy of an electoral campaign, to get an interview with Brando, the journalist Lawrence Grobel realized he'd won the part when he heard the actor grumble over the phone: "Listen, do you want to do this in Tahiti?"[90] The filming of *Bounty* changed Brando's life dramatically: after all, wouldn't these enchanting islands become his final resting place? The film bears the trace of this consuming devotion that was also the adventure of an era. Tahiti for Brando was at heart what

India had been for a whole generation of hippies: the discovery of an alternative culture and free love. The actor was taken with the white sands of Bora-Bora and the tranquillity offered to him by a population that had little interest in celebrity. He also succumbed to the customs of the archipelago, as did numerous crew members who acted out in real life the scenes from the film in which Westerners are excited about the beauty of the wahines. "'It was very confusing, and out of control,' said one staffer. 'You had girls getting pregnant and having to leave the cast, so they had to bring in new girls and shoot the scene again for continuity.'"[91] More than a film shoot, the crew's time in Tahiti resembled, according to all accounts, a permanent orgy.

In addition to the chaos that resulted, there were the staggering production costs. Tahitian women go bare-breasted, but in a flush of modesty the studio decided to hide their breasts with leis: a thousand of them were needed each day for all the extras! During the filming of the climactic scene of the British sailors arriving on Tahiti, the beach selected suddenly displeased the team of set designers because of its black volcanic sand. Disregarding the cost, they quickly covered it up with white sand hauled in from the other side of the island. And when Heimata "Charlie" Hirshon, a businessman hired to facilitate relations between the crew and the local population, decided to marry a Tahitian dancer, MGM paid for the party

and the costume designer conceived the wedding gown! The result: the budget for *Mutiny on the Bounty* climbed pretty quickly to the unbelievable sum of thirty million dollars (it would earn back only twenty).

An Epic and Costly Shoot

In short, the filming of *Mutiny on the Bounty* was one of those bigger-than-life shipwrecks that mark the history of cinema. Inevitably, the effects are felt in the film. After several months of filming, when only a third of it was in the can, the studio tried to impose a new working schedule on the director, Englishman Carol Reed, known to posterity for his famous *The Third Man* (1949). Reed refused it point-blank and handed the project over, not without a certain amount of relief, to an MGM veteran, Lewis Milestone (*All Quiet on the Western Front*, 1930). It's not surprising we should have the impression, when watching the film, of seeing the same freewheeling Brando from *Désirée*: Brando was given no more direction here than he had been by Henry Koster. He pursued his own goal, without worrying about crew changes or his costars' vision of the film. And if Brando got on board with this project, it was in hopes of dealing with the darker aspects of the mutiny, everything the Clark Gable version carefully left out. In the true—and highly exciting—story of the *Bounty*, the fugitives couldn't imagine returning to the country; their transgression of military law would have been punished by death there. Thanks to an error in the maps of the period, they found a sure refuge on the lost island of Pitcairn. The small group took up residence there and, with the six Tahitians who'd helped them flee and the eleven Tahitians kidnapped along the way, they led a life that was far from idyllic despite the beauty of the place. Internal rivalries, disputes, and acts of violence abounded. Fletcher Christian himself died in 1793, murdered by other members of the small community. The leader of the mutineers might have paid for his doomed attempt to establish an equal sharing of power between the Polynesians and the British. Here again we find a favorite theme of Brando's in "the struggle of black versus white, of good versus evil."[92] And we can imagine how much *Bounty* must have seemed to him at first a unique opportunity to tackle the themes he liked best.

Yet the sheer madness of the shoot, the innumerable affairs with local women and notably Tarita, his partner on screen, the attacks of bulimia, the drinking, the appalling relations he maintained with other actors all diverted Brando from his main objective: to make *Mutiny on the Bounty* a film with a message. He was uncomfortable with his character—his aristocratic origins seemed too much of a stretch to Brando, as did the English accent he had to adopt,

as usual with little success. Often distracted, he passed up the chance to alter the script and found himself forced to resort to his favorite policy in cases of extreme discontent: the boycott. Thus Lewis Milestone had to endure the two-faced game of his star, who whispered contradictory instructions to the director of photography, Robert Surtees. And to add to this joyful chaos, let's not forget that Brando as always took a devilish pleasure in undermining his costars. In one scene cut during editing where he had to slap Richard Harris—a big scrapper if ever there was one—Brando threw the actor off by reaching his hand out gently, as if he were going to stroke his cheek. "Thrusting his chin forward he propositioned, 'Come on, big boy, why don't you fucking kiss me and be done with it!' Brando glared back, white with rage. Harris then kissed Brando on the cheek and hugged him. 'Shall we dance?' Angry and embarrassed Brando stormed off and afterwards the two men refused to appear on the set together."[93] A pity, since the homoerotic subtext suggested here by Brando and the *Billy Budd*-like rereading of the relationship between Fletcher and Mills promised to be a fascinating nuance.

It was the same story when the studio, tired of the star moaning about the script, suggested he propose his own ending. Brando came up with the most anticlimatic ending imaginable. Fletcher Christian, hiding in a cave, watches the mutinous crowd of sailors pillage and rape the earthly paradise where they've found refuge. It was a good idea that offers a key to his performance: he is, above all, an observer, distant and ironic. Thus, in the first scene, we see from behind an unremarkable man walking—like all the gentlemen of his class, he sports a gray suit, a hat, and a cane. But if we look at him more closely, a few small details—an extravagant red cape, tight pants, and, hanging on each arm, a comely lady—indicate a kind of whimsicality. Where might this irresistible dandy be walking? In the park of a noble residence, among the richly adorned crowds on a posh street? Not at all: our friend Fletcher Christian is at the harbor getting ready to embark on an imposing Royal Marine ship, the HMS *Bounty*. When his captain asks him why he, a man who could easily lead a life of idleness and leisure, is heading out to sea, he answers with a smile, "You know, one must do something." Such is Fletcher Christian—insolent, nonchalant, irresistible. While around him restraint and the sense of duty reign, our man puts his pleasure before all else.

The Dandy and the Tormentor

Very soon after the *Bounty* has left port, Captain Bligh proves to be a sadist of the worst stripe, obsessed with corporal punishment, who doesn't shrink from murder as a way to impose his law.

For a long time, Fletcher Christian silently witnesses this deplorable spectacle. An innocent sailor is whipped for supposedly stealing provisions: Fletcher watches the scene without saying a word. The captain argues for harshness in every instance, whatever the gravity of the wrongdoing: overcome, Fletcher rubs his hand over his face without further opposing this intolerable talk. Ned (Tim Seely), a wittier sailor than the others, is sent up to the masthead for telling an impertinent joke: Fletcher pretends to laugh it off, hoping to hide from the captain how much he can be affected by the suffering of others.

Here again, the comparison with *One-Eyed Jacks* is revealing: Rio was a born actor, always performing—until love compelled him to be honest. Fletcher, for his part, is instinctively honest from the opening scene, where he makes no effort to mask his dandyism, his disinterest for his profession, and his lack of respect for hierarchy. But when it's a matter of survival, he finds within himself the resources of a consummate actor. All of Brando's greatness is due to the manner in which he makes us see the difference between these two attitudes: his sincere good humor in the opening scenes, his easy smile, his body's loose movements, give way little by little to a subtle state of tension. "Remember, fear is our best weapon," the terrifying Captain Bligh assures him. Fletcher does not respond, but with an eminently graceful gesture he envelops himself in his black cape. Because he's usually so still, a gesture from him constitutes a truly powerful reply. Moreover, impassivity is the key word for Brando's performance in the first part. When the captain orders the sailors to stop drinking water—in order to save the breadfruit trees, which are the whole reason for the expedition— a sailor dying of thirst falls while trying to go up to the masthead to retrieve the water ladle. Fletcher Christian is on the scene: he barely registers a jolt and slowly places his hand over his heart. Never before has Brando seemed such a minimalist.

A Reluctant Hero

While he satisfied his personal predilection, most importantly Brando touched upon the very essence of his character. For the Fletcher of this *Bounty* is not a great man by nature—which Clark Gable was in the first film—but rather a reluctant hero, who despite all his efforts can't resist his own goodness. In other words, Fletcher Christian comes across as an alien in the context of a big-budget epic. After all, for the first two hours of the film, the person every sign points to as the leader of the mutiny referred to in the title does absolutely nothing; he's content to observe, like an alter ego of the viewer, the monstrousness of Bligh. From then on, our interest in the character hangs on the turmoil we imagine going on in his head. "Must I act?" he seems to be asking himself the whole time. If not, how should he avoid taking action? A sailor is keel-hauled on orders of Captain Bligh. For a while, Fletcher seems to ignore the torture. He stays still, his eyes downcast. The dramatic change—which is inevitable, as it was in *One-Eyed Jacks*—takes place in a long sequence shot. The shot goes on and on. Suddenly, in one movement, he removes his hat. Then, after a moment, he puts it back on. Nothing happens in this shot, outrageously enough, nothing! And yet, it's impossible not to grasp that we're witnessing the metamorphosis of Fletcher Christian, mulling over thoughts that will end in mutiny. "[His] silences were often more eloquent than the lines he had to say,"[94] Kazan said of Brando quite correctly.

A few minutes later, the result of these evolving thoughts occurs on screen: a sailor who has drunk bilge water goes crazy and requires freshwater. Fletcher starts to give him some but the captain intervenes. Fletcher decides then to strike his superior! This will be the character's only moment of true violence. Later, when he puts Bligh in the launch that will carry him far away from those he's tortured for so long, Fletcher takes his whip from a sailor. A long static shot follows where Brando, still inscrutable, turns in front of his enemy with the whip in hand. Will he use it? We'd swear he will! Ah, but no. He slips it over Bligh's shoulder with surprising gentleness: "Take your flag with you." This refusal of the law of an eye for an eye and the character's profound goodness are a revelation. Fletcher seemed superficial, inconsistent, charming. He is in fact generous, deep, irreproachable. We thought he symbolized whimsy in the face of Bligh's rigidity, yet what he really represents is purity. While Rio embodied Christ scorned, Fletcher is the sacrificial lamb, he who—after long reflection—agrees to give his life for the common good. When his men congratulate him for having won, Fletcher, his face in shadow, exclaims, "Won? Won what, you damn fool?" He is well aware that, in his deed and in his fine altruism, a death wish can also be discerned.

Seduced by Maimiti

The same metamorphosis occurs in him with regard to love. The film's opening scenes present the character as a Don Juan for whom women are interchangeable. Everything changes upon their arrival in Tahiti, which gives rise to an incredible whirlwind of feelings. After being shut up inside the ship full of men, after the monotony of the sea and sky, we see the luxuriant vistas of the island open up, with its colorful crowd of inhabitants joyously singing songs of welcome. The very long scene where Maimiti (Tarita), the chief's daughter, welcomes the sailors with a dance is one of the most original scenes of seduction: her eyes riveted

on Fletcher, she seems to have chosen him in advance. Seated, Fletcher gazes at her with a sometimes amused, sometimes embarrassed air. He doesn't say a word or move a muscle. Though the camera lingers indulgently on the young Tahitian's swaying hips, it doesn't make Fletcher any less the true object of desire. What happens next will prove this: Maimiti will follow Fletcher wherever he goes, no matter the risk. Of course, if you're not upset by it, you'll smile at the terribly dated representation of the Polynesians as carefree and uninhibited creatures who know how to enjoy life's pleasures. The more the film exalts its "noble savages"—the wise old joker who is the tribe's chief; the gentle Maimiti, a veritable R & R on legs—the more condescending it seems. Only a few scenes manage, thankfully, to escape this trap.

Such is the case with Maimiti and Fletcher's first romantic embrace. Was this the result of the obvious chemistry between Tarita and Brando? The young woman, who doesn't speak a word of English, mispronounces the name of her suitor. He corrects her: "No, no, Fletcher." In doing so, he causes another misunderstanding. Now Maimiti is convinced the lieutenant's name is "No, no, Fletcher." This screenwriting trick works marvelously. For when Fletcher draws closer to the beauty to kiss her and she calls him "No, no, Fletcher," he has it easy, correcting her languorously, "Yes, Fletcher. Yes, yes, Fletcher."

Later, once the mutiny has been committed, Fletcher, demoralized, remains below deck aboard the *Bounty*, which has been partially deserted by her crew. He knows that by defying the authority of his superior he has reached the point of no return. Then Maimiti arrives to pull him out of his depressive apathy. The healthy anger the young woman expresses strips her of the vapidity that threatened to define her. Here she's energetic, passionate, and ready to do anything to save her lover. It might be the only example of this type of relationship in one of Brando's films: no romantic love, no violins, but rather a determined pragmatism, an iron will in the body of a nymph. Hence, perhaps, the authentic look of surprise that flashes across Marlon Brando's face at this moment in the film.

Nevertheless, it is not Maimiti who gives *Mutiny on the Bounty* its emotional force, but rather Fletcher Christian. Brando dreamed of a thought-provoking final scene in which his character would witness Evil taking over the world. He would end up getting a scene of sublime sacrifice. In reality, the mutinous refugees in Pitcairn set fire to the *Bounty* in 1790, as a convenient way to wash their hands of their crime. The same happens in the film, but for a very different reason: the men who secretly torch the ship wish to keep Christian from returning to England, where he wants to face his judges and restore his honor. Heedless

In 1966, Marlon Brando became the atoll of Tetiaroa's official owner—or more precisely its tenant with a ninety-nine-year lease granted by the French government. In this small paradise of fine sand on a turquoise sea, protected from trespassers and the media curiosity he was subject to, the actor could daydream at his leisure. Would he set up an artists' commune or a nature park? In the end, despite numerous projects, Tetiaroa would remain simply a place of residence for Brando, who—by filming *Mutiny on the Bounty* and then marrying a Tahitian— put French Polynesia on the world map. And since the tremendous upsurge in tourism on the archipelago is largely attributed to him, it seems to make sense that they've announced the opening of a luxury hotel called simply "The Brando."

Lieutenant Fletcher Christian, a sailor and decided dandy.

of the flames, Fletcher strives to retrieve the sextant that will allow him to sail home, despite everything, and he's brought back to land only after he's been seriously injured. Lewis Milestone directed this scene with a consummate sense for the dramatic: instead of showing Fletcher's face as he leaves the ship, he first films the reactions of terror and suffering of those around him. When Fletcher's finally shown lying on the Pitcairn shore, it is in semidarkness, unprecedented in a film that for the most part takes place under the most blinding of suns.

At times disoriented—"What's happened, Brown?" he suddenly worries—at times philosophical—"Bligh left his mark on all of us"—Fletcher lies dying, his eyes full of tears. As in that critical scene where he removed and replaced his hat on the bridge, just before rebelling against Bligh, Brando doesn't play an action hero here but rather a thinking man. And he shows us, in passing, what plays out in the mind of a dying man. After having lived through mental torture and physical pleasures without betraying a single emotion, after having maintained a haughty impassivity for so long, Fletcher loses control. His face trembles, his teeth chatter. "Am I dying, Brown?" His voice is soft, almost surprised. "What a useless way to die!" This long scene, which strongly resembles an operatic aria, contains an endless range of nuances: Fletcher's vulnerability, his fear, his natural dignity, his

generous heart. And his declaration of love for Maimiti rings true: "Please… please know that… that I… I loved you more than I knew, and if I only had time to… to…" He trails off, his eyes fixed. And then death takes him.

7

Major Weldon Penderton

Reflections in a Golden Eye (1967)
John Huston

"Any fulfillment obtained at the expense of normality is wrong and should not be allowed to bring happiness."
—Weldon Penderton

A shadow hangs over *Reflections in a Golden Eye,* that of Montgomery Clift, the only actor Brando ever truly admired. The idea of adapting Carson McCullers's short novel[95] for the screen actually came from Clift's agent, Robbie Lantz, who wanted to fulfill Elizabeth Taylor's wish to work again with her closest friend. Ever since *A Place in the Sun* (George Stevens, 1951) it was clear Liz and Monty were practically twins or, better, soul mates—they both had alabaster skin, jet-black hair, and big blue eyes as well as the same mischievous and wounded spirit. Their deep, unfailing bond had once pulled Clift from the jaws of death: during their infamous car accident in 1956, Elizabeth Taylor had saved his life by pulling out with her bare hand the teeth that, smashed in by the impact, had lodged in his throat and threatened to choke him. When the McCullers project began, Clift—despite his prestige among directors of his time—hadn't made a film in four years. Since his dreadful accident, he was addicted to innumerable painkillers and was a serious alcoholic, and everyone in the business knew it too well. Who could forget that the oranges he'd sucked on during the filming of *Suddenly, Last Summer* (Joseph L. Mankiewicz, 1959) were soaked in vodka? "Nobody was sure Montgomery Clift could act anymore. Monty wondered himself,"[96] Patricia Bosworth recounts in her biography of the actor. But Elizabeth Taylor overcame these obstacles with her steady determination. She convinced a revered filmmaker, John Huston, to direct this triangle of unfulfilled desires. She fought the reservations of the producers, who of course worried about the script's provocative nature: it concerns a Southern military base where a respectable major in the American Army lusts after a private, who is himself obsessed with the major's ravishing spouse. After all, homosexuality remained a major taboo in American cinema. But no one opposed for long the formidable Miss Taylor, who at thirty-three was the world's biggest star. Robbie Lantz would later recount how much she "was determined to have [Monty] in *Reflections* and to make another picture with an actor she admired greatly and loved as a friend, and her immense devotion to him was not only responsible for the acceptance of Clift by John Huston, [Taylor] also overcame certain insurance problems."[97]

Brando Replaces Montgomery Clift

When filming began in the fall of 1966, however, it was without Montgomery Clift: he had succumbed to a weak heart in July just before turning forty-six. Following the tragedy, Brando agreed to take up the role of Major Weldon Penderton, even though he'd always tried to avoid the theme of homosexuality—probably out of fear of his own ambiguity. This act of courage is explained primarily by the complex and passionate relationship, a curious mixture of rivalry and boundless admiration, that Brando had with the deceased. Toward the end of the 1940s, Clift nearly lost his status as reigning prince as soon as Brando, four years his junior, burst onto the Broadway stage. Energetic, sensual, and provocative, Elia Kazan's young protégé was the opposite of Clift, the refined and modest intellectual whom *A Place in the Sun* had made a star. Nevertheless, they were regularly offered the same parts; for example, Clift had turned down the role of Napoleon in *Désirée.* Kazan even thought about bringing them together on the same marquee in Steinbeck's *East of Eden* (1955), with Brando in the role of Cal, the rebel, and Clift as Aron, the favorite son. A dream cast, even if the refusal of the two stars gave Kazan the chance to discover James Dean. Audiences and critics compared them constantly and the two actors themselves became obsessed with each other. Clift was convinced audiences preferred Brando over him: "It's a chemical thing. Marlon connects more immediately with an audience than I do."[98] He admired his magnetism and went to see each of his films, eager to understand how his younger peer "shows you what is going on inside himself."[99] In his memoirs, Tennessee Williams recalls the brilliant Clift of 1946 who was "the most promising young actor on Broadway, this being a couple of years before the astonishing advent of Brando, which I suspect had much to do with the long and dreadful crack-up of dear Monty."[100] Brando, for his part, sought to emerge

Marlon Brando as Major Weldon Penderton in John Huston's *Reflections in a Golden Eye* (1967).

109

**Montgomery Clift
(1920–1966)**

It was to his exceptional beauty[c] that Montgomery Clift owed his debut as an actor. A model since childhood, on stage at fourteen, he was deeply influenced by his work with the most famous acting couple of the period, Alfred Lunt and Lynn Fontanne, who taught him the essentials of their technique. Thus, like Brando, Clift wasn't really a product of the Actors Studio—he took classes there when he was almost thirty. He also worked largely with the same directors as Marlon—Fred Zinnemann, Elia Kazan, Joseph L. Mankiewicz, John Huston, and Edward Dmytryk. For *Wild River* (1960), Kazan would've preferred Brando—who'd been giving him the cold shoulder since *On the Waterfront*—to portray Chuck, a government official in Roosevelt's administration sent to convince the inhabitants of a small Tennessee

valley to leave their homes, which are threatened by the construction of a dam. The macho Kazan ended up with an angst-ridden Clift, weakened by his dependence on alcohol and pills. But Monty's performance, admirable in its subtlety, ultimately served the intentions of the director, who contrasted the intense vulnerability of his antihero with the earthy strength of the female characters. A form of virility different from that of the classic gloating Hollywood male is what characterizes Montgomery Clift on-screen, and without his homosexuality— which caused him a lot of suffering—being the principal explanation for it. The plots of *A Place in the Sun* (George Stevens, 1951), *I Confess* (Alfred Hitchcock, 1953), and *Suddenly, Last Summer* (Joseph L. Mankiewicz, 1959) thus put Clift's character in

the center of a dilemma that allows him to express moral anguish, far from the purely instinctual impulses of Kowalski or Terry Malloy. That's why Clift found himself being offered the roles of intellectuals—in *The Misfits* (1958) as in John Huston's *Freud: The Secret Passion* (1962)—that remained beyond Brando's reach. His premature death put an end to a life haunted by self-loathing as well as to the competition that pitted him against the only actor of his generation he admired, Marlon Brando.

from the shadow of Kowalski. He took care over
his appearance, his choice of reading material,
and his circle of friends, without ever managing,
despite all these efforts, to project the same aura
of intellectual refinement as Monty. The difference
was that Clift didn't have to play cultivated
dandies: he was one at heart, a man of letters keen
on Russian literature, and especially Chekhov.

The two idols of a generation found themselves
working together in Edward Dmytryk's *The
Young Lions* (1958), but shared the screen only
briefly and without exchanging a word during the
final scene where Clift impassively witnesses —
should we read this symbolically? — Brando's
death. "I can tell you right now that if I had ever
had Montgomery Clift and Brando in the same
scene, that would have been the end of the picture
because their way of working was completely
opposite,"[101] the director assures us. Clift had liked
Irwin Shaw's novel, which focuses on three
characters: Christian, the Nazi officer (Brando);
Noah, the heroic Jew (Clift); and Michael, the
American terrified by the war (Dean Martin).
But Dmytryk's adaptation hardly pleased him,
especially since it modified the character of
Christian to satisfy Brando's heroic aspirations.
On set, Brando came to observe Clift work and
tried in vain to hide behind the camera. "Tell
Marlon he doesn't have to hide his face when
he watches me act,"[102] Monty told his director.
One day, Brando asked to speak to his older

costar in private and revealed what he thought
of him: "You're what I challenge myself against.
Take care of yourself for me so that you can keep
challenging me because you're all I have."[103]
But Montgomery Clift did not take care of
himself, and when shooting for *Reflections in
a Golden Eye* began, Marlon Brando found
himself with no one to challenge him and no one
to revere. It's hardly surprising that when he was
approached to take up the role of his secret idol,
he felt a measure of inner torment: "He wasn't
sure about the part," Huston recounts in his
memoirs. "He had read the book, but doubted
his suitability. As we were talking about it, the
final screenplay was being typed, so I suggested
that he wait and read it. Marlon did so, then took
a long walk in a thunderstorm. When he came
back, he said simply, 'I want to do it.'"[104] What
followed was a stunning performance in which
Brando gave himself up to his own vulnerability
like never before.

Unfulfilled Desires, Frustrations, and Perversions

Yet the moment Major Penderton appears on
screen, he's giving a demonstration of his strength.
Dressed in a white T-shirt with his dog tags
around his neck, he's lifting what appear to be
extremely heavy weights. Concentrating intensely,
his face contorted with the effort, the major looks
at himself in the mirror and flexes his biceps.

There's no doubt: here is a man of action whose well-toned body itself looks like a weapon. We then find Penderton, no longer alone in his room and out of view but in uniform, facing the dashing Private Williams (Robert Forster), whom he orders to do some small gardening tasks. His tone is neutral, his face impassive. It's the same when he lectures to a class of young soldiers: Penderton wears his uniform like a suit of armor that protects him from any outside intrusion. Only his look betrays him, sometimes fixing for a long moment on Williams, whom he desires, or on his wife, Leonora (Elizabeth Taylor), whom he hates. We then see him go over to Leonora, who is curled up on a hammock with a glass in her hand. Penderton walks upright, displays perfect politeness, and complies when she asks him to spell a word. And he does all of this without ever looking at her. Instead he turns his head away; he has eyes only for Williams. Having done the work poorly, Williams is reprimanded by the icy Major. Leonora, though, is no dupe. She keeps her eyes riveted on her husband and swings in her hammock, lascivious and mocking. "Firebird is a stallion," she says with suspicious insistence. Penderton lifts his eyes to her but still avoids looking at her. Yet her line hits its mark: he freezes, turns his back on her, and leaves.

This long scene allows Brando and Elizabeth Taylor to suggest at once the sexual frustration that smolders between the Pendertons, all the complexity of a marital relationship unlike any other—with unfulfilled desires, mutual humiliation, and suppressed sadism. All this is present in every instant of Brando's performance, for example, in the scene where the Major, in his office, is irritated when he hears his wife's laughter coming from the kitchen, where she's with the maid. He moves toward the door, closes it at first, and then, after standing still for a moment, opens it again, determined to go complain. The tension in his entire body and Brando's contained violence reveal all of his character's torments. Once in the kitchen, Penderton looks at his watch and corrects the wall clock. His movements are measured, precise, suggesting that if he gave in to any more spontaneity his world would be turned upside-down. When Leonora leaves the kitchen, her husband's eyes settle on her for the first time in the film, and it is not a good thing. "You look like a slattern going around the house this way. […] You disgust me," he says. Leonora smiles, as if the insult were just the compliment she was waiting for. Then, with a defiant air, she undresses and throws her bra in Penderton's face while he looks on, mute and impassive. The masochist has finally met his sadistic match, and Brando a costar on his acting level. "To me, [Brando and Clift] tap and come from the same source of energy […] they both have the vulnerability," Elizabeth Taylor would say years later, slipping in an "Oh God. Marlon will kill me!"[105] even though from her, this was the highest compliment.

The beauty of Marlon Brando and Elizabeth Taylor's *pas de deux* in *Reflections in a Golden Eye* is due to what each of them knows to hold back and give up. Taylor masters perfectly the art of saying horrible things in a playful, sometimes even tender, tone. She also knows that, given the malaise Brando expresses, her sensuous beauty alone is provocative. And Brando, rightly, isn't satisfied just to show inhibition or control. At times, he cracks. Thus at the unbearable sight of his naked and indifferent wife climbing the stairs with exquisite slowness, he grips the banister with unspeakable rage and screams at her, "I'll kill you. I swear, I'll kill you! I'll do it! I will kill you!" She silences him with a single line that is at once a threat and a domineering erotic promise, delivered in a fresh tone: "Son, have you ever been collared and dragged out into the street and thrashed by a naked woman?" Penderton remains speechless, his mouth twisted in rage, his eyes fixed, his hands clenched on the banister. Then his chin trembles, he bows his head, and, subjugated, he crumbles. Because he has given in to despair, Brando then returns for a long moment to his initial impassivity. Leonora plays cards with her lover, another military man, while her husband serves her a drink. Lieutenant Colonel Morris Langdon (Brian Keith) comments: "Weldon, your wife's cheating," a *double entendre* signifying both "at cards" and "in her marriage." It is a pointless provocation since Major Penderton remains indifferent, his face neutral and his voice controlled. It takes a shrewd observer to recognize the crushed and humiliated man from the previous scene.

The Major's Torments

John Huston perfectly re-creates the suffocating atmosphere of the novel. The film is tinted with a yellow that dulls Elizabeth Taylor's big violet eyes and makes even the exterior shots terribly claustrophobic. The characters all observe one other in silence, and their comings and goings are regularly interrupted by the shot of an eye whose iris reflects the action. It is the eye of the peacock painted by the young Filipino houseboy Anacleto (Zorro David), who says: "Look! A peacock. A sort of ghastly green… with one immense golden eye. And in it… these reflections of something tiny and… tiny and…" Alison (Julie Harris), Colonel Langdon's wife, completes his thought: "Grotesque." Thus she provides the key to the metaphor of the title. For the sight of the perversions and the hatred of this small group of characters is also reflected, perhaps, in the eye of that incorrigible and silent voyeur, Private Williams. We see him watch Major Penderton from behind while, seated at his desk, he examines old photographs taken from a cardboard box. Since the Major's back is to us, our eyes naturally go to the subtle movements of his hands, which hold the photos or polish a small spoon wrapped in black cloth. Brando's natural body language is easily recognized, but we also know he uses it only if it fits the role. Here, the contrast between the major's physical strength, broadcasted in his first appearance, his rigidity, and the feminine gentleness of his movements of course reveals his character's inner contradictions. There is a range of other nuances in the scene where the major finds his wife asleep, and in all likelihood drunk, before the chimney. He takes her in his arms, carries her upstairs, lays her on the bed, and then undresses her. Brando strips his movements of all sensuality; they are technical, functional, mechanical. Once he's put his wife, deserted and voluptuous, to bed and she finally lies still, he lifts his hand to his temple. Here again, the familiar tic: Brando likes nothing more than to touch his face to suggest a character's moment of introspection. Except that here, his hand, wearing a spectacular ring, strokes his head as if to signify that the major's amorous urges are primarily directed at himself.

It makes sense, then, that the film's most surprising moments, those that reveal the most unfamiliar Brando, show Penderton alone with himself. For example, when Private Williams breaks into the house at night for the first time, unbeknownst to everyone; just before showing the soldier picking the Penderton's lock, Huston inserts a shot of the major lying in bed. The sheet is turned down over his chest, and his hand lies on his heart. Brando manages to convey the major's restraint and inhibition even in the most unguarded moment: during sleep. Toward the end of the film, he applies cold cream in front of the bathroom mirror, until he looks like a sad clown. Earlier, we saw him—still being spied on by Williams—speaking to himself in a mirror. His words are indistinct, and all the better. Our attention is thus drawn to his unbelievably expressive body and eyes. Penderton salutes himself, gives a large smile, then becomes serious again. The smile is especially chilling: it's his only smile in the film and it offers us a projection of the man Penderton could be if life didn't so systematically destroy his deepest aspirations. A striking *mise en abyme* since Major Penderton practices being a respectable soldier the way an actor would, in front of his mirror. He watches himself without the least distance, as if he truly were someone else. Julie Harris told Peter Manso that Brando "seemed to love the part, and you felt he had a great deal of empathy for this man. There was nothing campy about it. He was taking the role seriously, almost as if he was exploring his own sexuality, or his own inner torment."[106] In fact, this encounter with the mirror is remarkable for the sincerity of Brando's acting, his total absence of distance. He suddenly seems a male Blanche, in the end not far from what Pedro

Almodóvar had in mind when he said that *Streetcar* should be performed with a man in the role of Miss DuBois.

The Major Loses Control

Most of *Reflections in a Golden Eye* takes place inside, and when the characters do go out, it's always to ride a horse. Horses here symbolize sexual freedom: Leonora is a skilled rider who is practically in love with her stallion, Firebird; Langdon is a fair if unimaginative rider; as for Private Williams, he rides his mare bareback, completely naked. That leaves Major Penderton, who obviously fears horses, falls off on the first jump, and ends up with his face in the dirt, only to be subjected to his wife's jibes. On the set of *Reflections*, Brando was never difficult. The man who usually so enjoyed manipulating his partners, being cruel to directors, or throwing tantrums that called attention to him, showed himself to be extreme kind. But he suffered from anxiety, especially when he had to shoot the horse scenes: "I wondered then, as now, if Marlon got this fear because he had so immersed himself in his role. The character he played had a fear of horses,"[107] John Huston would later remark. The climax of the film—in other words, Major Penderton's ultimate humiliation—happens, incidentally, because of a horse, the precious Firebird, who represents for Leonora everything her husband fails to be: a stallion that never disappoints her. One morning the major decides to ride it, alone, and without asking for his dreadful wife's permission. The horse his wife strokes like a lover. Here he is saddling and bridling it with mechanical precision, just like that he used when handling the sleeping Leonora. Very soon, the horse bolts, jolting Penderton's restrained body like a rag doll, as branches strike his face and splatter it with blood. Thus, it's on a mad horse, with any pretense of control forgotten, that Weldon passes the object of his secret love, Private Williams, sitting naked in the woods. No wonder he falls! Clinging to the reins, he lets himself get dragged a few yards by the wild Firebird, then he breaks down.

Yet this loss of control is nothing compared to what follows. Weldon stares at Firebird in horror. It is the same look he gave the naked and nasty Leonora at the beginning of the film. The aggressiveness with which he whips the horse is meant for none other than her. It must be underscored how much this scene of cruelty toward an animal is uncommon in Hollywood film, where it's usually reserved for evil antagonists or bad guys in B movies. Huston revisits here a motif from one of his prior films, *The Misfits* (1961), in which a certain Montgomery Clift played an essential role, but he goes further here than that film, in which the cruelty toward horses sparks the passionate

Top: Horses are everywhere in the film. Here, Langdon (Brian Keith), Leonora, and Penderton—the lover, the wife, and her husband—take their regular horseback ride.

Bottom: It's with his wife's horse, an enraged Firebird, that the major loses control and gets dragged along on the ground for several yards.

intervention of Marilyn Monroe. Here, the more miserable of the two is not who we think it is. After savagely beating Firebird, Major Penderton, horrified, opens his eyes wide and weeps, his face in his hands. This is perhaps the most moving moment in Brando's entire career. These tears, these groans of pure pain emerge from a valorous soldier who must face the obvious: he has lost his war against himself. We're a long way from the punishment inflicted on Rio in *One-Eyed Jacks*, which was sought out, accepted, and deliberate. Weldon is far more helpless: his masochistic impulse, and the violence he inflicts on himself, have caught him off-guard. It is during this moment of absolute vulnerability that Williams appears. The soldier, who has no idea he's the catalyst of the drama, walks by the major without so much as a glance and takes Firebird by the reins to lead him back to the stable. Back at the house, Penderton's lacerated face and lost expression arouse little compassion in Leonora. "You say he ran away? Is he loose? […] Well, how is he? […] Are you sure he's all right? […] Any cuts on him?" she asks before running to the stable. Like a warrior goddess in her white robe, pleated in the Greek style, Leonora reappears in the doorframe, riding crop in hand. Next to a small group of military men—including her lover who is giving a lecture on the United States—her husband is silent as always. "So Firebird's all right, is he?" she asks. And she lashes his face.

Never mind that Marlon Brando's filmography abounds with masochist scenes, the raw and spontaneous violence of this moment is astounding. Brando remains impassive, his eyes frozen, his chin high, preserving the dignity of his character in spite of everything. "He stood like a statue. He did not defend himself," Anacleto tells Alison in the following scene. And yet at no moment would we dare say that is Weldon passive: his acceptance of the punishment has, to the contrary, all the depth and intensity of action. While giving his military strategy lecture, the major asserts: "Now a man does not flee because he's fighting in a unjust cause. He does not attack because his cause is just. He flees because he's the weaker, and he conquers because he's the stronger." Yet Penderton himself has merely stood his ground. Is he the weakest because he's ravaged by the torment of his homosexual urges and humiliated by a jealous woman? Or the strongest because he has the strength not to desert the field of battle? This magnificent ambiguity transforms the lecture into an inner monologue. "Leadership," he explains with his eyes lowered, totally ignoring his attentive audience, "must include a measure of inherent ability to control and direct self-confidence based on initiative, loyalty to superiors, and a sense of pride." Pride is not an easy word for Major Penderton, who speaks

of it with restrained rage in his voice. His face is so sorrowful when he takes the lectern and brings his hands together while lecturing about leadership that you'd think he was about to cry.

The Mistake

The more *Reflections in a Golden Eye* moves toward its tragic conclusion, the more the major is shown to be incapable of retrieving the degree of control he'd previously attained—before his escapade with Firebird. While his wife and Colonel Langdon play cards, Penderton breaks an object on the mantel and suffers a rebuke from Leonora, who dryly invites him to become an enlisted man again, to live away from the disorder he constantly complains about. "Of course you're laughing at it, but there's much to be said for the life of men among men… with no luxuries, no ornamentation. Utter simplicity. It's rough and it's coarse, perhaps, but it's also clean. It's clean as a rifle. […] They're seldom out of one another's sight, and they… eat and they train, and they shower and they play jokes and… go to the brothel together. They sleep side by side. […] There are friendships formed that are stronger than… stronger than the fear of death. And they're never lonely. They're never lonely. And sometimes I envy them," Weldon responds. Huston asked Lawrence Grobel whether he remembered this scene where Brando speaks about the army, standing in front of the chimney. "[…] It's a long speech and he fiddles with a candle. Well, after the first time I could have said, 'That's it,' as I often do; but knowing Marlon and the way he works, I said, 'Let's do it again.' We did it three times, and each time was different; any one of them could have been used. […] I've never seen another actor do that."[108] True, this long speech has the force of a theatrical soliloquy, delivered as if just for himself as he stares into space. This dream of male camaraderie—which would conceal a form of love—finds such free expression because, at that moment of the story, Penderton believes Williams is secretly watching him… and therefore loves him silently in return. The same evening, he prepares for Williams's arrival, alert to the sound of the front door, and waits with a neck stiff and bated breath. Huston keeps Brando's face in darkness since there's actually no point in showing us his eyes wide-open in suspense, his trembling desire. He's felt these emotions at every instant throughout the film.

When Williams arrives at the top of the stairs and enters Leonora's room, a light illuminates Weldon's face. From then on, he knows: he's not the one Williams lusts after, nor the one he comes to contemplate each night while hiding in the shadows. He waits a moment then goes to get his pistol, opens the door and shoots the soldier who, seated on the floor, gazes at his sleeping wife.

After having fired, he brings his hands to his head.
Thus ends the tragedy of Weldon Penderton, the
solitary and cursed lover. And with it, the most
astonishing performance of Marlon Brando,
one in which he faces the shame-filled part of
his character with poignant innocence. What
greater homage could he have paid to ontgomery
Clift than showing the torments of a homosexual
racked with guilt, surrounded by a hostile
world that condemns his desires and rejects them?
"Yet his work was so beautiful and so pure,"
Julie Harris would later say of Brando's work
in *Reflections*, "that there was no explaining
where it came from. He still didn't love acting,
he didn't love the theater and he didn't respect
his own talent, but his gift was so great he couldn't
defile it. He could put on pounds, he could say
that it was all shit, but he still couldn't destroy
it."[109] On set, like Williams circling the Penderton
house, there prowled another actor, Richard
Burton, then married to Elizabeth Taylor.
Fascinated, hypnotized even, by Brando, he went
to the set to watch him act. And he noted in his
journal, "He has depth. It's no accident that he
is such a compelling actor. He puts on acts of
course and pretends to be vaguer than he is.
Very little misses him as I've noticed."[110] History
repeats itself: Brando loved to watch Clift; Burton
observed Brando, who acted in honor of Clift's
memory... And who knows what golden eye this
endless merry-go-round is reflected in?

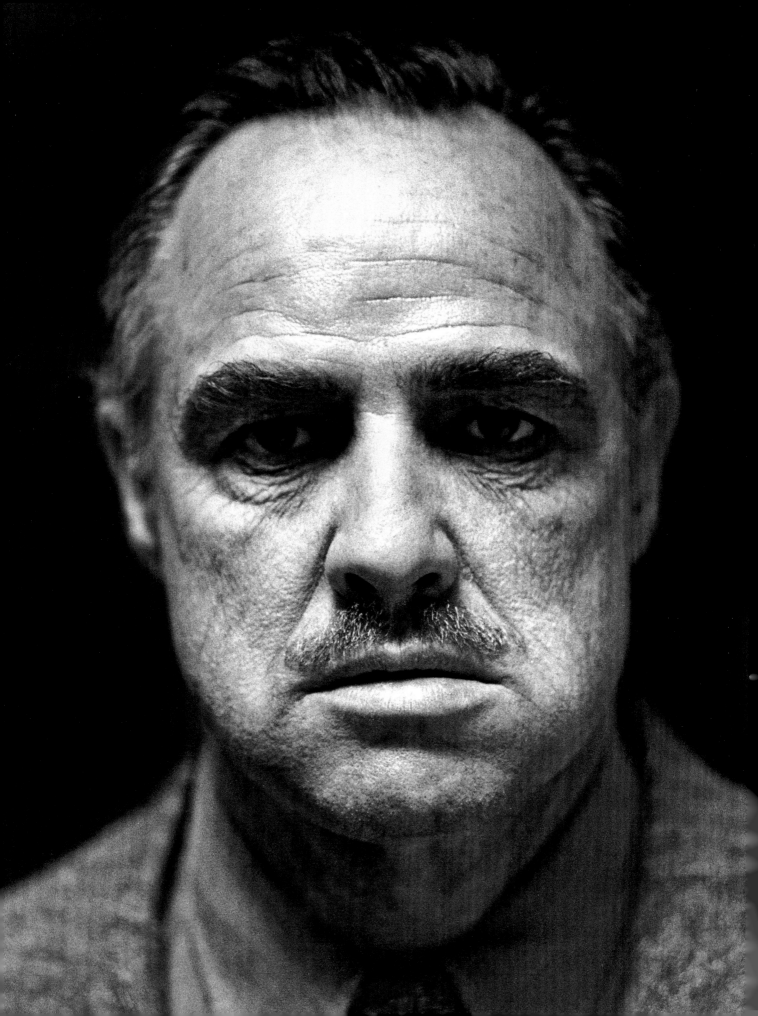

8

Don Vito Corleone

The Godfather (1972)
Francis Ford Coppola

"I worked my whole life. I don't apologize for taking care of my family. And I refused to be a fool, dancing on a string held by all those big shots."
—Don Vito Corleone

It was one of those Hollywood meetings like so many others, a match fought with pulled punches under the guise of urbane politeness. In one corner, Francis Ford Coppola, a young filmmaker, barely thirty years old, bursting with energy and very proud of his handful of barely seen films, was getting ready to enter the big league with an adaptation of Mario Puzo's bestseller, *The Godfather*. In the other corner, two industry heavyweights, Albert Ruddy and Stanley Jaffe, president of Paramount. The director's youthful enthusiasm left the two producers cold. Coppola was obsessed with the idea of making Marlon Brando his Don Corleone, betting that "The mystique Brando had as an actor amongst other actors would inspire precisely the kind of awe in working with the legendary Brando and would translate on film into awe for the powerful godfather."[111] But his wish to give the role of an old Italian mafioso to Brando, then forty-seven and with ten years' worth of duds behind him, seemed ridiculous to the producers! Not only was Brando the wrong age, and not at all of Sicilian descent,[112] but he'd recently lost much of his prestige by making film after film, and so many of them bad. Who remembers *Bedtime Story* (Ralph Levy, 1964) or *The Night of the Following Day* (Hubert Cornfield, 1968)? In his filmography from the last few years, there was hardly anything salvageable except, of course, *Reflections in a Golden Eye*—a commercial flop—*The Chase* (Arthur Penn, 1966), a contemporary Western manhunt in which he played but a supporting role, and *A Countess from Hong Kong* (1967), an odd film, sure, but one directed by Charlie Chaplin all the same. In 1970, when casting for *The Godfather* began, Brando had just finished *Candy* (1968), a psychedelic farce directed by his friend Christian Marquand, and *Burn!* (1969), memorable mostly for the tales of its hectic shoot and for the bloody confrontation between Marlon and director Gillo Pontecorvo.

Brando, Obviously

Here's how Ruddy and Jaffe hoped to dissuade Coppola from his casting choice: Yes, Brando was once a genius, but lately he'd become a moviemaking machine and an impossible one at that, always late and hungry for money. In short, Jaffe concluded formally, it was simple: "As president of Paramount Pictures, I assure you that Marlon Brando will never appear in this motion picture." Then in a dramatic turn of events, Coppola curled up into a ball… and fell to the floor, apparently stricken with convulsions. Picture the scene, the civilized discussion that preceded it, the classy producers in suits, the eloquence of young Coppola, who lived only for his film and who pleaded as if his life depended on it. And then, suddenly, everything was upended, the conversation interrupted by screams, the negotiation hijacked, the office abruptly transformed into a theatrical scene. "My 'epileptic fit' was obviously a gag, but they got the point. Finally they recanted and told me I could consider Brando."[113] Translation: for the first time since *Julius Caesar*, Brando had to do a screen test. A challenge, Coppola told himself, since film hadn't interested the man in ages. How would he convince him to prepare for the part? Then the real miracle happened, because, for the first time in many years, Marlon Brando was determined to take on a role. As it turned out, Brando was as adamant as Coppola: he really wanted to play Don Corleone.

Was it because, after many years of being in a rut, he finally found himself faced with a real challenge? "I've always felt that you can't ever play a part that's either bigger than you are in personality or so far a reach for you that you fall on your face. I had no frame of reference to play a sixty-five-year-old Italian,"[114] he would explain when the film came out. But Brando was passionate about makeup, about artifice. That was exactly what had pushed him, fourteen years earlier, to accept the role of a Japanese character in *The Teahouse of the August Moon* (Daniel Mann, 1956). When Coppola came to shoot the screen test in his house on Mulholland Drive, he saw the actor come out of his bedroom in a kimono. Brando quickly put on a shirt and jacket, drew on a black mustache with shoe polish, and

To play the role of Don Vito Corleone in Francis Ford Coppola's *The Godfather* (1972), Marlon Brandon invented a bulldog mug for himself.

stuffed his mouth with paper tissues, explaining that the Godfather should look like a bulldog. And when he improvised some dialogue with Salvatore Corsitto, the Italian hairdresser Coppola had recruited to play Bonasera, the funeral home director, he invented a high–pitched voice inspired by notorious gangster Frank Costello. Coppola must have been amazed. Even more surprising than the inventiveness Brando displayed even before shooting began was the respect he showed his director. Throughout a grueling production schedule, during which the studio nearly fired Coppola four times, Brando consistently stood by the young filmmaker. When the latter had to fight again to insist on Al Pacino as his Michael Corleone, Brando called Robert Evans, one of the producers: "Listen to me, Bob. He's a brooder. And if he's my son, that's what you need, because I'm a brooder."[115] During the shooting, some of the crew—including the editor Aram Avakian— plotted against Coppola, but Brando declared loud and clear that he wouldn't continue working on the film without him. This was proof of the young filmmaker's authority since, according to *The Godfather*'s director of photography, Gordon Willis, "If Marlon feels there's one controlling factor on the set, he won't screw around. Where he gets out of hand is if no one is in charge. It's as if he's seen the hole in the boat and he panics."[116]

And so, in Coppola's competent hands, Brando took immense pleasure in making this film, which came along to distract him from some serious personal problems—his son Christian's descent into drug abuse at the age of only thirteen, his sister Jocelyn's uncertain health, the innumerable lawsuits that set him against his ex-wives and some disgruntled former employers. On the set of *The Godfather*, he was a living god, as Mario Puzo would later recount, feared and admired by a troupe of young men full of talent and mischief— James Caan, Robert Duvall, John Cazale, and Al Pacino. He liked playing affectionate, intimidating father types, and loved it when Coppola asked the Corleone clan to gather on their days off to eat together and improvise, in short, to fuel their onscreen relationships with real experiences. Caan and Duvall, eager to attract their teacher's attention, took inspiration from his famous pranks to devise various displays of buttocks and ways to swipe his prompts—since Brando no longer learned his lines but read cue cards hidden around the set. Of course, there were bad days as well, those when an anxious Brando called on Coppola for endless discussions about his character. The rule was simple, almost mathematical, as the filmmaker eventually understood: "when Brando was half an hour late, he complained about a specific line. An hour late and he claimed not to understand a scene. If half a day late, the

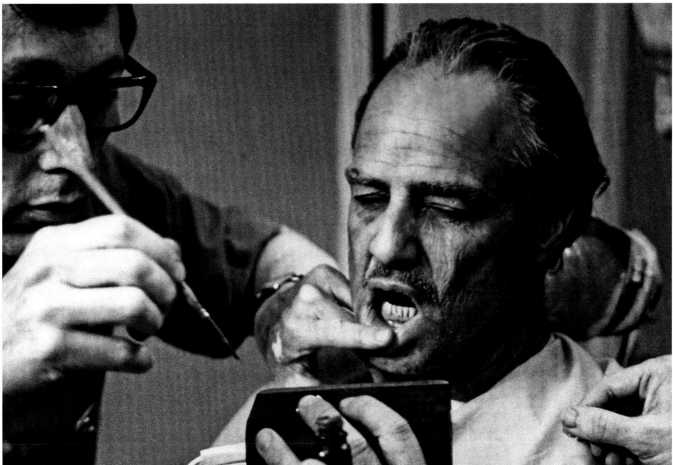

explanation became, 'I don't like this scene at all.'"[117] But for the most part, the mood was one of joyful camaraderie. Brando made a few memorable jokes — like the sudden mooning he gave, which took everybody by surprise the day they shot Connie's wedding, or when he added weights to his gurney, making it impossible to lift him during the scene where the old Don is brought back home from the hospital.

To these schoolboy pranks were added other childish pleasures: those of makeup and disguise. The brilliant Dick Smith — previously responsible for Dustin Hoffman's metamorphosis in *Little Big Man* (Arthur Penn, 1970) — created an oral prosthetic for Brando to replace the Kleenex he'd used in his screen test. It really gave him the look of a bulldog with heavy jowls. Every morning, Smith re-created Don Vito's sagging skin. As his partner Philip Rhodes explained: "I pulled and stretched his skin out, then Dick painted rubber on it. When the rubber was dry, I let the skin fall back into its relaxed position, and the rubber wrinkled up so that we could highlight and shadow the wrinkles."[118] He still had to come up with the gait of an older man: ten-pound weights placed in his shoes helped to slow down his movements. A true professional, Brando worried about the effect on screen. Gordon Willis told Peter Manso, "His concern — and rightly so — was that with all that age makeup, he had to be lighted properly or it would look like shit. I knew that if I simply put light directly in front of him, the effect of the makeup would be neutralized. So I had to come up with the kind of lighting that would not only be right for him, but also right for the rest of the movie. I explained this and he immediately understood. He seemed to have an intuitive grasp of what had to be done technically and how to function within those limitations. […] He was aware of having to determine how big or small the field size of the screen would be, and he adjusted his movements accordingly. From that first makeup and lighting test, I saw that he had a very attuned sense of visual containment."[119]

The King in Action

Perhaps it's this visual sense, which speaks to his profound understanding of filmmaking, that reveals the true reason Brando invested himself in the role of Vito Corleone: he understood he was making a great film. Fixated on the American experience — obsessed with the massacre of the Indians, captivated by Westerns — he could not have missed, from the moment he read the screenplay, the power of the metaphor at play in *The Godfather*. "I believe in America," says Bonasera by way of introduction. And all that follows will be the patient, methodical deconstruction of this declaration of faith. The mafia here is not an absurd and reprehensible deviation, but rather a means of exposing the inner workings of society as a whole. Don Corleone's not just one of many gangsters; he's a portrait of a patriarchal figure of Shakespearean dimensions who holds in his hands senators and policemen, studio heads and industrial leaders, everyone the country considers respectable. "I always thought of *The Godfather* as the story of a great king with three sons," Coppola liked to say about his film.[120]

So it's a king that Brando portrays, an enlightened and frightening monarch, unpredictable and loving, who combines the cruelty of Stanley Kowalski with the kindness of Terry Malloy. From the famous opening scene, we sense and are unsettled by the Godfather's double nature. Coppola refrains from showing him as long as possible, filming Bonasera close-up and in the dark as he recounts his story — how his daughter was beaten and nearly raped by two Americans, who were immediately let off by the courts — and very slowly lets us see the back of Don Corleone's head and his right hand ordering Sonny with an expressive gesture to give Bonasera a drink. "Why did you go to the police? Why didn't you come to me first?" the Godfather asks, still seen from behind, in his rasping voice. For the first time in his career, Brando's famous mumbling didn't bother his director: "Powerful people don't need to shout,"[121] Coppola explained, captivated by the wheezing, whispered voice the actor had invented for the role during his audition. But let's return to Bonasera, who remains anxiously deferential. He approaches the venerable Don Corleone to whisper in his ear his greatest wish of seeing his daughter's aggressors die. It's then that we see the Godfather's face for the first time. Gordon Willis's lighting plunges his eyes in darkness, so that it's impossible to read his expression. "The idea was that this was a character who didn't always let you know what he was thinking,"[122] explained the director of photography, who was heavily criticized by the producers during the shoot but later acclaimed for this brilliant idea.

It's true we don't know what he's thinking, but we certainly see what he's doing. While reprimanding Bonasera for his lack of respect — "I've known you for many years, but this is the first time you've asked for help" — he pets a small cat nestled in his lap that lets him play with it with his hand. A sign that with those weaker than him, Vito is gentle, attentive and even affectionate. Except that the cat's also a feline and its presence can be read as a metaphor of the character's savage nature, a distant memory of Stanley's dreadful caterwaul in *A Streetcar Named Desire*. The moment Bonasera — who has yet to understand the rules of the game — asks him how much he must pay to have his revenge carried out, Don Corleone gets up and sets the cat on his

Bonasera (Salvatore Corsitto) comes to ask Don Vito to avenge his daughter.

Following pages: Don Vito still looking sharp in his dark suit, giving orders, imposing his authority, and enjoying the devotion of those around him.

The Godfather:
Opening Scene

Marlon Brando subtly changed the dialogue written by Mario Puzo and Francis Ford Coppola, notably in the famous opening scene. A comparison of the two versions allows us to assess just how critical a role he played in the creative process of *The Godfather*.[d]
Screenplay: "Then take the justice from the judge, the bitter with the sweet, Bonasera. But if you come to me with your friendship, your loyalty, then your enemies become my enemies, and then, believe me, they would fear you…"
Film: "Bonasera… Bonasera… What have I ever done to make you treat me so disrespectfully? Had you come to me in friendship, then this scum that ruined your daughter would be suffering this very day. And if by chance an honest man like yourself should make enemies, then they would become my enemies. And then they would fear you."
Screenplay: "Some day, and that day may never come, I would like to call upon you to do me a service in return."
Film: "Some day, and that day may never come, I'll call upon you to do a service for me. But until that day—accept this justice as a gift on my daughter's wedding day."

Like a good father, Don Vito Corleone waits for his son Michael (Al Pacino) to arrive before immortalizing the wedding day of his daughter Connie (Talia Shire) in a photo.

Opposite: Brando embodies a respected patriarch, imbued with natural authority and unexpected tenderness.

desk. "Bonasera, Bonasera. What have I ever done to make you treat me so disrespectfully?" He waits, patient and implacable, for the undertaker to bow before him and kiss his hand while calling him "Godfather." Indeed, Brando does play a king, one who knows how to make others pay allegiance to him without ever raising his voice or making a threat. Once satisfied, he makes a gesture of agreement and leads Bonasera out by the shoulder. "Give this to Clemenza. [...] We're not murderers, in spite of what this undertaker says," he murmurs to Tom Hagen (Robert Duvall). And he smells the flower he's wearing in his lapel.

All of Brando's choices—the voice, the cat, the flower—move in the same direction: toward an unexpected gentleness and sensitivity in his character. Which means he doesn't have to make an effort to appear frightening or dangerous. Is it due to his star status? The myth that surrounds him? He exudes such inherent authority, such prestige, that the reverence all the minor characters show him appears natural to us. After Bonasera, it's a baker who comes to ask him to prevent the deportation of his future son-in-law, an illegal immigrant. Vito agrees and the man grabs both of his hands in a surge of enthusiasm: "You understand everything." Outside, the party is in full swing and Luca Brasi, a hatchet man who has asked to be received by the Godfather, is rehearsing his speech: "Don Corleone, I'm honored and grateful that you have invited me to your home on the wedding day of your daughter…" Brasi's nervousness was shared by the actor who played him, former fighter Lenny Montana, who was terrified at the idea of making his screen debut in a scene with Marlon Brando. He repeated his lines over and over in a corner of the set and thus gave Coppola the idea of including the scene in the film. We must wait for another scrounger, the crooner Johnny Fontane (Al Martino), for the violence in Vito to become palpable. Once again in his office, two fingers on his cheek, he listens to his distraught godson. He's lost his voice, and he needs a role to get himself back on top—here you'll recognize Brando's former rival, Frank Sinatra, around the time of *From Here to Eternity*.[123] "Godfather, I don't know what to do. I don't know what to do," the crooner concludes, holding his head in his hands. The Don suddenly jumps up, with the ease of a young man, and shakes him, shouting, "You can act like a man! What's the matter with you? This how you turned out, a Hollywood *finocchio* that cries like a woman?" Here is Vito Corleone's violent side, his unpredictable temper. Though he seemed old and peaceful, he's as quick as a cat, and cruel at that: suddenly, his face falls, and he pretends to whine loudly—"What can I do? What can I do? What is that nonsense? Ridiculous!"

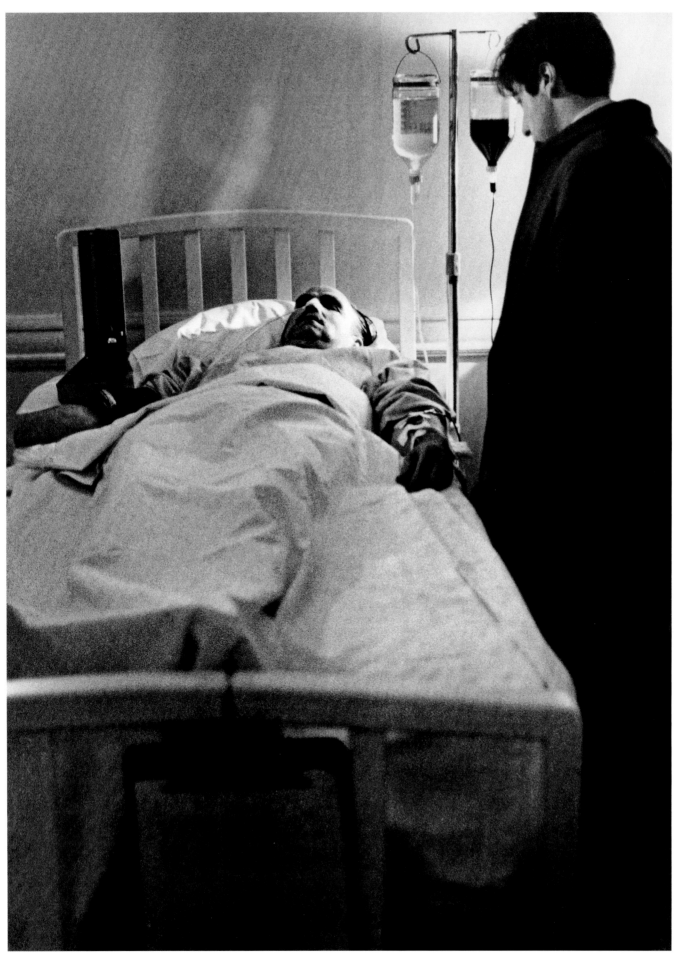

He finally calms down, as quickly as he flared up, promising Johnny a solution to his problem. "I'm gonna make him an offer he can't refuse," he says, accompanying him to the door and embracing him. The storm has passed.

There is the Godfather, the man in the shadows, who arranges extortions and executions in the privacy of his office. And there is Don Vito Corleone, the head of the family, who jokes with his wife, worries about not having his whole clan around him, and who waltzes with his daughter the bride. In all of these little scenes from Connie's wedding — images awash in laughter and sunlight — Brando retains the imposing severity of the look, the aura, of power. But he softens his steps and allows himself some more relaxed movements, more graceful poses. Never mind his jowls and his wrinkled skin: as he takes Connie (Talia Shire) by the hand, waves to the crowd, and then jokes with her, giving her the big smile of a loving father, the charm takes effect and it's a good-natured and tender figure we see. This aspect is the ingredient that makes *The Godfather* such a masterpiece: it's not only a harsh commentary on the true nature of American society but also a family drama. Brando's tortured soul, his hypersensitive emotionality, makes him a father we immediately recognize as both loving and loved. Robert De Niro, given the role of the younger Vito in *The Godfather Part II* (1974), would not forget this dimension of the character: we see him sitting up at baby Fredo's crib, applying cupping glasses with anxious tenderness.

The End of a Reign

Even if you know the film by heart, when you rewatch *The Godfather*, the brevity of Vito's reign is still surprising. The beginning of the film has barely shown us that he's an emperor, the king of the New York Mafia, when he is shot. While his son Fredo waits behind the wheel of a car, Don Corleone shops for fruit on a street in Little Italy. He points out what he wants to the grocer, his gestures slow and measured. When he spies two suspicious characters advancing toward him, he wants to flee; he runs, but his steps are too heavy, his breath too short, and he collapses on the hood of his car, hit by their shots. The Godfather slowly rolls over and falls on the ground. His eyes are closed, his face distorted by pain. Highly theatrical, the fall Brando stages at this moment in the film errs on the side of being unrealistic, and yet has a tremendous effect on the viewer. It follows a meticulous three-step choreography that allows Brando to bring the scene to a moving conclusion and, consequently, to underscore its meaning: the great and powerful Don Corleone ends up flat on his back in the gutter, like a wounded wildcat. We recognize here the sure instinct for melodrama that Brando's always had:

most often minimalist, he also knows that a touch of grandiosity is sometimes necessary. We must wait for the very end of the film to see Don Corleone die, and when he does, it will be quietly, as if by accident. What plays out here, in front of the Mott Street greengrocers, is something different: a symbolic death, the end of one reign and the promise of another.

What's more, when we see Don Corleone again, he's in a hospital bed, with his son Michael, the future monarch, watching over him. Vito is lying with his eyes closed, attached to an IV drip, in a state of absolute powerlessness. Concerned that another assassination attempt might take place that Christmas night, Michael asks a nurse to help him move the bed. "Just lie here, Pop. I'll take care of you now," he whispers to his father. Vito blinks his eyes to show that he's understood. Michael gently strokes his father's head and kisses his hand. And Don Corleone, smiling, lets tears stream down his face. It is a key moment of the film, both unusual and precious. During Connie's wedding, we saw that Vito attaches particular importance to his son Michael: there's no way the family photo will be taken without him, and from his office, as he takes care of his sinister business, Don Corleone watches Michael's arrival out the window, peering through the blinds.[124] But afterward, it's Sonny and Tom we see always at his side taking care of business with him. The hospital scene gives us all at once a sense of the strength of the love that unites the father and son, a love expressed in their words and gestures, in the tenderness of the one's impulses and the other's obvious emotionalism. If Al Pacino and Marlon Brando hadn't managed to make us feel this, *The Godfather* wouldn't have the same force. For in this mysterious and ancestral bond, we find the real reason behind Michael's dramatic change. Michael, the good son, the decorated soldier, he who was going to lead the Corleones to legitimacy, assures his fiancée (Diane Keaton) that it's not him, it's his family. After the hospital scene, that same Michael will become the new Godfather, ready to kill and to return to his Sicilian roots, all to honor one single promise: "Just lie here, Pop. I'll take care of you now."

The Godfather and His Sons

Yet the son's metamorphosis devastates the father. When Don Corleone finally returns home, his face haggard from exhaustion, and he learns that it was Michael who killed Sollozzo, he shakes his head and closes his eyes, wrenched by inexpressible sorrow. In the scene preceding his death, during a long conversation in the garden with Michael, Vito is more explicit: "I knew that Santino would have to go through all this. And Fredo… Fredo was, well… But I never wanted this for you. I worked my whole life. I don't apologize for taking care of my family. And I refused to be a fool, dancing on a string held by all those big shots. I don't apologize. That's my life, but I thought that… that when it was your time you would be the one to hold the strings. Senator Corleone. Governor Corleone. Something." Written during production by screenwriter Robert Towne, whom Coppola had called in to help, the scene is deeply moving. It plays on the broader theme of the film — the Don became a mafioso to counterbalance the power of those who hold the strings, the politicians, and hoped his son would take the logical next step by becoming one of them. It also expresses all the complexity of a father–son relationship, with its expectations and its inevitable merging of identities: moreover, Brando and Pacino are each filmed in profile, as if to suggest two versions of the same man. It makes us sense the time that has passed since the start of the film and the glory days: here, Vito is an old man who has gaps in his memory and the irresistible tenderness of a grandfather. When Michael, who appreciates the dream of legitimacy that he will not stop pursuing, assures him they'll get there, Vito takes his son's face in his hands and kisses him on the cheek. And then he warns him: "Now listen, whoever comes to you with this Barzini meeting, he's the traitor. Don't forget that." As in the scene of his death — he puts orange slices in his mouth to scare his grandson before collapsing among the tomato plants — Brando underscores constantly how much Don Corleone's emotionality, his love for his family, is inseparable from his dangerousness. He just wanted to have some fun with the little boy by making himself look like a monster, and he ends up terrifying him. He just wanted to secure a future for his sons by controlling organized crime on the East Coast, and he ended up destroying their lives.

The most moving scene in *The Godfather* occurs earlier in the film, when the death of Don Corleone's son Santino ("Sonny") is announced. Late at night, while everyone's asleep, the Godfather joins Tom Hagen in the living room. This is long after Connie's wedding, where Vito looked dapper in his dark suit with a flower in his lapel. Here he's disheveled, his hair's a mess, and he's wearing pajamas and a bathrobe, with a scarf wrapped around his neck. Until now, we've seen him giving orders, imposing his authority, and enjoying the devotion of those around him. But this evening, he's the one to implore, in a whisper, his eyes infinitely sad, as if he already knew tragedy has struck: "My wife is crying upstairs. I hear cars coming to the house. Consigliere of mine, I think you should tell your Don what everyone seems to know." Tom must make a superhuman effort to obey him: "They shot Sonny on the causeway. He's dead." At that moment, Brando has a lost look, as if he'd just received a physical shock. He lets out a soft sigh, a hoarse groan. He raises his eyes to stop the tears from falling: "I want no inquiries made. I want no acts

In *The Godfather Part II*, Robert De Niro plays the young Don Vito Corleone.

Robert De Niro as
Don Vito Corleone
(*The Godfather Part II*, 1974)

For anyone who wonders about Marlon Brando's legacy, *The Godfather Part II* offers a fascinating case study. Here we see a thirty-year-old Robert De Niro in Don Corleone's shoes. "[…] De Niro's face reminded me of Vito Corleone," said Francis Ford Coppola. "Not of Brando, but of the character he played with the accentuated jaw, the kind of funny smile. De Niro certainly is believable as being someone in the Corleone family and possibly Al's father, as a young man."[e] It wasn't actually a matter of playing the same character, but rather the same man, only younger. Instead of trying to do an imitation—which would have been risky since the two men are nothing alike—De Niro had the intelligence to draw upon the older Vito's repertoire of gestures and expressions: "I watch him and I say, 'That's an interesting gesture. When could he have started to do that?' It's my job as an actor to find things I can make connections with. I must find things [in *The Godfather*] and figure out how I can use them, in what scenes I can use them to suggest what the older man will be like."[f] And, indeed, De Niro reproduces Brando's gestures—he touches his face, keeps his silence, remains impassive. And he shares moments of unexpected tenderness: as when little baby Fredo is sick and Vito soothes him.

of vengeance. I want you to arrange a meeting... with the heads of the five families. This war stops now." His voice breaks during that last line. He gets up and goes to Tom, who's still seated and who leans against him, rubbing his back. "Call Bonasera. I need him now." Don Corleone heads down the hall with painfully heavy steps. We see him with the undertaker. "Well, my friend, are you ready to do me this service?" He approaches the body, which is covered with a black sheet. "I want you to use all your powers and all your skills. I don't want his mother to see him this way." He very slowly raises the sheet. He looks at the body and whispers, in his small, fragile voice, his face distraught: "Look how they massacred my boy." In that instant, it's no longer about the Mafia or crime fiction, games of power or an actor's *tour de force*: we are in the presence of pure grief, that of a man who has lost his son and who cannot help but feel responsible.

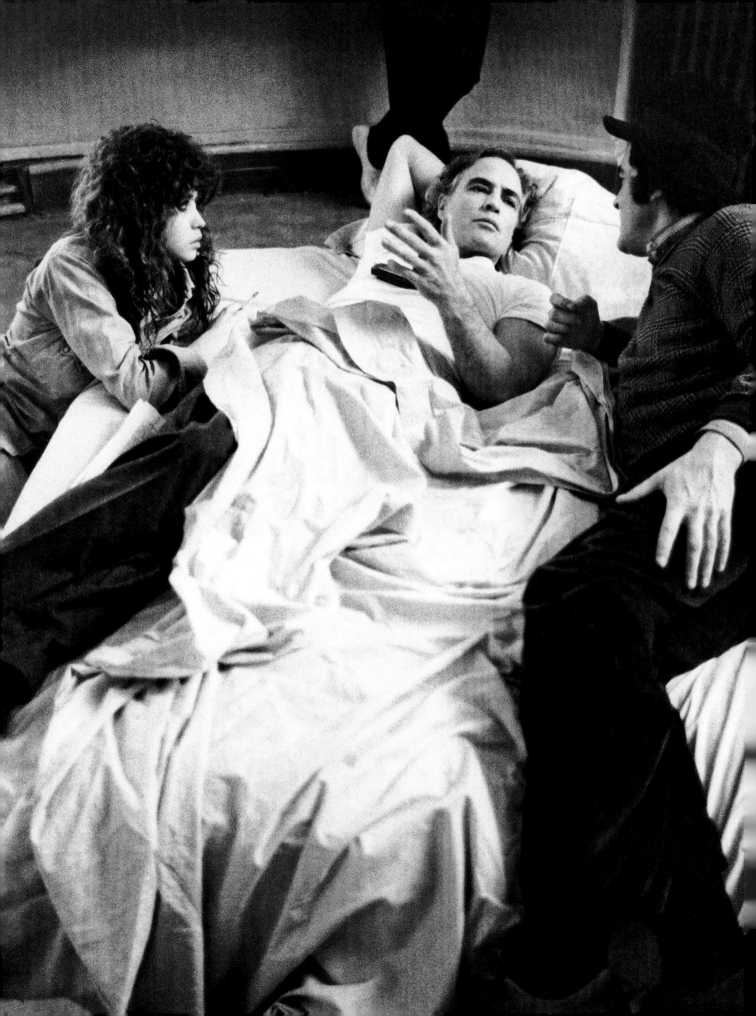

9

Paul

Last Tango in Paris (1972)
Bernardo Bertolucci

"We don't need names here. Don't you see?
We're gonna forget everything that we knew."
— Paul

In the opening credits of *Last Tango in Paris*, two paintings by Francis Bacon are shown on the screen. A man, a woman: a single flesh, pitiful and contorted, a single despair. "Why Brando?" people would constantly ask Bernardo Bertolucci years after the release of their one and only legendary film, which forever carries a whiff of brimstone. Because of Kazan, he would sometimes say, or even because of the overwhelming memory of *Julius Caesar* or *Reflections in a Golden Eye*. Occasionally, when he was in a good mood or he trusted the interviewer, he would reveal the true reason: it was this painting by Francis Bacon representing "a man in great despair who had the air of total disillusionment"[125] that immediately conjured before his eyes the unmistakable, even tragic, image of Marlon Brando. Did he ever mention this to Brando himself? Did Brando at once grasp how well the young Italian filmmaker was able to see his inner turmoil without shrinking, without ever falling for the virtuoso game of his charm and intimidation? Whatever the case, from the moment they met, Brando let down his defenses. As if by magic, their first meeting transformed into two-weeks' worth of daily conversations that fulfilled the order issued by the director from the very start: "Let's talk about ourselves — our lives, our loves, about sex. That's what the film is going to be about."[126] Bertolucci summed up what he discovered about the star in a few words: "There is an element of wild, irrational violence in him. If you can enter into his universe and harness this intuition and violence, then he becomes incredibly intelligent."[127] Above all, he made a film out of it.

A Very Personal Role

For those who love Brando, no film — except *One-Eyed Jacks* — compares to *Last Tango in Paris*. This is because Bertolucci chose to turn away from the magnificently well-written scripts that up till then had made him a success (*Before the Revolution*, 1964; *The Conformist*, based on the novel by Moravia, 1970). Because, in doing so, he allowed Brando the man to reveal himself

on screen. And because the director and his actor established a totally new kind of relationship, different from the filial bond that had made Brando's films with Elia Kazan and Joseph L. Mankiewicz powerful. A twin-like relationship, perhaps, where each man could recognize himself in the other and that liberated Brando from his self-loathing, his inhibitions, gradually leading him to reveal his true self. Of course, the film's subject — the destructive sexual affair between a man and a woman who know nothing about each other — demanded the complete immodesty of the actors. Maria Schneider, not yet twenty years old and with only a few minor roles under her belt, bares all with no apparent concern, and only later, after years of going through hell, would she say how much it took out of her. Brando himself hardly exposes his body. In his partially improvised exchange with Marcel (Massimo Girotti), his dead wife's lover, he asks the handsome aging man: "What do you do about your stomach? That's my problem." But in the film, his stomach is always concealed either by his clothes or by Maria Schneider. Unlike his young and more vulnerable costar, Brando was protected by his director. "It is also possible," Bertolucci would say, "that I had so identified myself with Brando that I cut [a scene where he's naked] out of shame for myself. To show him naked would have been like showing myself naked."[128] Long improvisation sessions led him to divulge whole swaths of his life — childhood sorrows, unrequited loves, his masochistic urges, his self-loathing. When the elevated metro passes over him on the Bir-Hakeim bridge, Paul plugs his ears, shuts his eyes, and howls. A long howl of pain, so poignant he impressed even the director during the shoot: "Maybe I cannot work at the level of this actor."[129] This scream defines the tone of the film: a character's primal scream that comes to life onscreen and that each viewer is free to interpret as he or she wishes — even though some do hear "Fucking God!" This incoherent scream is also a note of grief that the character will hold until the final collapse. Moreover, when a pretty girl, Jeanne (Maria Schneider), walks by and then glances back at him, Paul doesn't even notice her. Absorbed in himself, focused on his despair, he expresses such distress that we'd swear he's about to break down in tears. Before this Brando has portrayed many an instant of despair, and he's

Beneath the Bir-Hakeim bridge, Marlon Brando (seen here with Bernardo Bertolucci) plays Paul, a widower who cries out in grief.

Opposite: In an empty apartment, Paul meets Jeanne (Maria Schneider), with whom he will have a perverse erotic relationship over several days.

played them well. But this is the first time he must portray it continuously, without variation and especially without any hope of it coming to an end.

Shortly after having passed him on the bridge, Jeanne sees Paul again in a nearby café: he's leaving a phone booth. Bertolucci films his expressionless, inscrutable face in an extreme close-up, and the look Jeanne gives him is fascinated, eager, already enamored. Again it's him she finds in an empty apartment that she'd like to rent and that he's also viewing. Slumped against a wall in the fetal position, he doesn't respond to her "Who are you?" Yet once she's walked around enough, with an attractive nonchalance, he asks her, authoritatively despite his faltering French, "Do you like it?" Her: "I don't know. I have to think about it." Him: "Think fast." Surprise! Here again we find Napoleon—the Napoleon of *Désirée* who merged the language of love with military commands. Brando had finally gotten his hands on the perfect script for this brilliant concept, and it wasn't a Hollywood romance with pasteboard sets but rather a pure erotic encounter, stripped of all sentimentality. Indeed, it had nothing to do with knowing whether the young woman with the hat liked the dark and empty apartment. Paul approaches Jeanne, throws off her hat, carries her over to a shuttered window, and rips off her panties, and they have sex standing up before collapsing on the floor. What's surprising here is not so much the frankness of the scene—scandalous

in 1972, terribly banal forty years later—but its naturalness, the blatant urge, immediately satisfied, that we see on-screen like a logical consequence of the desperate howl in the beginning. After finishing, Paul remains stretched out on the floor, flat on his stomach, with his face in his hands.

Paul's secret is soon revealed to us. When he gets back to his place, in a seedy hotel he manages, he finds the caretaker, Catherine (Catherine Allégret), washing the bloodstained walls of the bathroom. She recounts what she said about him to the police, who came to question her about his wife's suicide. Looking out the window on the other side of a glass partition, Paul ignores what she's saying. So who is this American that wanders Paris like a lost soul, this bereaved husband? "Do you know that he was a boxer? […] It didn't work out, so he became an actor, a bongo player, a revolutionary in South America, a journalist in Japan. One day, he lands in Tahiti, hangs around, learns French. Then he comes to Paris. There he meets a woman with money, marries her, and…" If we still had doubts about there being parallels between the actor and his character, here they are all laid to rest. You'd think it was an inventory of Marlon Brando's roles and biography: the boxing comes from *On the Waterfront*, the Mexican Revolution from *Viva Zapata!*, the reference to Japan from *The Teahouse of the August Moon* or *Sayonara*. Bongos were always a passion of Brando's, and as for Tahiti, we know the story! Besides these indirect references,

Brando and his character are both haunted by suicide. Brando's mother, Dodie, alcoholic and profoundly self-destructive, tried to end her life several times. Much more than his relation with Jeanne, it's Paul's grief, anger, and sadness that give *Last Tango* its force. That's when Catherine hands him the razor that Rosa, his wife, used to open her veins. Paul grabs her violently, taking her by the wrists and then by the neck, almost strangling her. "Yes," Catherine gasps, "she had cuts there… And on her neck, too." Later, Rosa's mother shows up at the hotel and sets off an incontrollable rage in Paul. "But I don't want any priests here. […] No priests." And because his mother-in-law keeps insisting, he throws her suitcase against the wall screaming: "The Church doesn't want any suicides, do they?" When she asks him why Rosa killed herself, he punches the door twice. It's a peculiar anger that Brando expresses here, very different from what he's performed up until then in that it's stripped of any control or demonstration of power. His body bursts with energy that doesn't know how to find expression; his voice trembles with feelings he cannot admit to himself. And the large amount of improvisation in the film leads us to ask what we're seeing. Is this a baffled actor who no longer knows what to do? A man overwhelmed by his own emotions? A brilliant portrayal of a person in distress?

We see the same ambiguity in the scenes with Maria Schneider. When Jeanne wants to tell him her name, Paul cries out in English (he's spoken only French up until then), "I don't have a name. […] I don't want to know your name. You don't have a name and I don't have a name either. No names. Not one name." He covers her mouth with one hand and pins her against the wall with the other. "You and I are gonna meet here without knowing anything that goes on outside here." The situation continues to the point of exhaustion like an exercise in a theater class. Paul's exasperation, when Jeanne asks him for the umpteenth time why, sounds like that of an actor who's tired of still having to repeat the same thing: "Because we don't need names here! Don't you see? We're gonna forget everything that we knew." Paul's antics strongly resemble the notoriously obscene jokes Brando would play on set. At the end of the film, in the tango ballroom, he treats even the dancers to his favorite trick: a public mooning. He's as mischievous as a kid. When Jeanne suggests she invent a name for him, Paul and Brando merge again—"Oh, God, I've been called by a million names all my life," he says wearily, and it's very much the response of a star who has played dozens of roles and been the subject of thousands of articles. After that, Bertolucci seems to leave Brando entirely to his own devices: he films him walking around the apartment, at loose ends, playing with every object he gets his hands on—the rung of a ladder he twirls in his hand, a lampshade through which he takes a deep breath. As we know, it's one of Brando's habits to spice up his scenes

with unexpected choices, but his strong silhouette, his haggard face signal the disarray, more than that of his character, of an actor who doesn't know what to do. When Maria Schneider finds him on the floor eating cheese, she mocks this experimentation that proceeds so precariously with welcome irony. "Do you really think that an American sitting on the floor in an empty apartment eating cheese and drinking water is interesting?" Brando agrees adamantly. Yes, it's interesting.

In retrospect, Maria Schneider would later express her deep bitterness about her memories of the filming of *Tango*, but at the time she got along fairly well with Brando, claiming when the film came out that she looked at him—despite their likely affair—"like a father figure." Bertolucci's assistant director, Fernand Moszkowicz, confirmed that "Brando and Maria had an excellent relationship, though. He was helping Maria in the scenes she found difficult to do…"[130] This involvement, although limited by their obvious differences in age and status, is perceptible on the screen in the rare moments, both affectionate and sincere, where Paul gently teases Jeanne and especially when he finally confides in her. After having noisily refused to reveal his name, Paul, against all expectation, brings up the reasons why he won't return to the States. With his face turned toward the camera, he begins to speak after a long silence. His voice is monotone, his eyes fixed. First there's his father, "a drunk." Then his mother, also "always drunk," who sometimes ended up in jail. Brando's parents' alcoholism was one of the things in his life that made him suffer the most, a demon that haunted him anew when his son Christian became drug dependent. "One of my memories, when I was a kid, was of her being arrested nude. We lived in this small town. Farming community. We lived on a farm. And I'd come home after school and she'd be gone. In jail… or something. And… I used to have to milk a cow every morning and every night and I liked that. I remember… One time I was all dressed up to go out and take this girl to a basketball game. And I started to go out and my father said, 'You have to milk the cow.'… So I went out and I was in a hurry and didn't have time to change my shoes. And I had cow shit all over my shoes." Recounting this humiliation, Brando—or Paul, it's impossible to tell—blinks his eyes and furrows his brow. His voice remains neutral, but his face betrays an intense and poignant emotion. He also mentions his mother: "My mother taught me to love nature. … I guess that was the most she could do… In front of our house we had this big field… And we had a big black dog named Dutchy. She used to hunt for rabbits in that field… And it was… very beautiful." Rambling and nostalgic, this monologue has all the qualities of a true confession that hasn't been worked out and takes the viewer by surprise. You could swear Elia Kazan was thinking of this very moment when he praised in his memoirs "the actors [who]—whether by technique or by

Marlon Brando's attraction to roles in which he's mistreated or humiliated is obvious well beyond the ten films studied here. Thus, in the remarkable *Fugitive Kind* (Sidney Lumet, 1959), his character, Val, a drifter who has an adulterous affair with a married woman played by Anna Magnani, is lynched by an enraged mob. Another lynching—an extraordinarily brutal one—takes place in *The Chase* (Arthur Penn, 1966), in which Brando, as sheriff, arouses the wrath of the townspeople. The character survives, but the actor's bloodied face and mangled body almost make us forget the violence of *One-Eyed Jacks*. The sexual dimension of Brando's taste for suffering is apparent before *Last Tango* in *The Nightcomers* (Michael Winner, 1971), a failed "prequel" to *The Turn of the Screw* by Henry James. Of course Peter Quint, the perverse valet Brando plays, displays mostly sadistic tendencies in his affair with Miss Jessel (Stephanie Beacham). But it's very much masochism that the actor showed by offering up his naked body and his tears in such a flagrantly low-end movie.

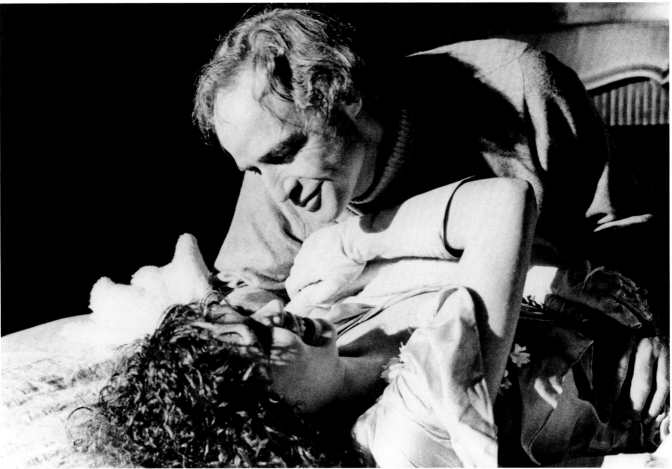

accident—gave you pieces of their lives, which is certainly the ultimate generosity of the artist, and they did it unabashed. You were the witness to a final intimacy. These artists spoke to your secret self, the one you hide. They offered you more than cleverness or technique: they gave you the genuine thing, the thing that hurt you as it thrilled you."[131] In *Apocalypse Now*, when improvising for Coppola, Brando would once again reveal his passion for a now irretrievable countryside, pure and unadulterated, inevitably idealized since it belonged to the inaccessible realm of his childhood.

A Pervasive Cruelty

And Paul has never quite resolved to leave that realm. Moreover, it was no coincidence he found Jeanne attractive: she's a kid, a barely mature Lolita who enjoys proclaiming, in all the innocence of her twenty years, that "Growing old is a crime." What she shares with her lover appears to be a perverse kind of recreation, in which each of them invents something to amuse them. She plays Little Red Riding Hood, he the Big Bad Wolf: he transforms the fairy tale's lines into dirty jokes. She suggests they come without touching each other. He makes animal noises that just about make her die laughing. When she thinks she's seen a rat and screams in fear, he pretends to catch it and eat it with relish: "I gotta get some mayonnaise for this. It really is good with mayonnaise." Even if

the oedipal dimension of their relationship became the subject of numerous commentaries, Paul and Jeanne are basically kids who, in the shuttered darkness of their large, empty apartment, hide from life for fear it will catch up with them. From childhood, Paul has also retained a terrible savagery. When his mother-in-law's hand seems too close to him, he asks her to move it, and when she doesn't, he bites it. Then he punishes her by playing an awful trick on her, cutting off the electricity in the entire hotel and sneering, with unremitting irony, "She's afraid of the dark. Oh, poor thing. All right, sweetheart. I'll take care of you. I'll give you a little light." Nothing's more terrible than Brando's gaping grin when he's pretending to be kind. In general his smile is vaguely disturbing—since it contradicts his sad gaze—but then he lets out a few genuine laughs, those of a sadist at the height of his pleasure. In fact, the erotic affair with Jeanne abounds in scenes of cruelty. Cruelty toward her, first and foremost. He apes her French accent, mocks her manners, ignores her declaration of love. To which we must add the famous butter scene, which in fact is really a rape: he pins her on the floor, ignores her tearful pleading, and sodomizes her as he lectures her about "where the will is broken by repression…" But he also exerts this cruelty on himself. Paul and Jeanne's relationship is a headlong flight, the expression of a terrifying death wish. After the rape, Bertolucci cuts together three shots of Brando

The Monologue in
Last Tango in Paris

"Go on tell me something.
Go on, smile, you cunt!
Go on, tell me... tell me
something sweet. Smile
at me and say I just
misunderstood. Go on, tell
me. You pig fucker! You
goddamn, fucking, pig-
fucking liar! Rosa... I'm sorry,
I... I just can't, I can't stand
it... to see these goddamn
things on your face... You
never wore makup. You
know... this fucking shit...
Take this off your mouth...
You always... lipstick...
Rosa, I... Oh, God! I'm sorry.
I don't know why you did it.
I'd do it, too, if I knew how.
I just don't know. God... I
have to find a way... [...]
What? [...] Oh, I... I'm
coming... I have to go. I have
to go, sweetheart, baby.
Somebody's calling me."

lying on the floor in different positions: here's Bacon's painting again, with its cloying sadness and its loathing of the flesh. When Jeanne declares her love for him, he tells her to put her fingers in his ass and, as she does this, he describes a fantasy where she's fucked by a pig that vomits on her face and then she drinks it. Back at his hotel, he nabs the john of a decrepit prostitute who, sensing his desire's faded, has taken off. Paul hits him, kicks him, throws him against a wall, and screams at him. Maybe because the prostitute confessed to being an old friend of "Madame Rosa." Or maybe because he sees in this pathetic man, with his pitiful desires and his typical cowardice, an unbearable replica of himself.

The Monologue in the Room

Yes, Paul is a masochist, like Rio, Weldon Penderton, and so many others characters played by Marlon Brando. A tormented soul who scorns his desires as much as his gifts, a suicidal person who, unable to do away with himself, compels those who cross his path to assist him. All this is brought to light in the most beautiful scene of the film, one in which Paul stealthily enters the room where the dead body of his wife lies, surrounded by suffocating violet flowers. Brando later laughed at the admiration this scene would earn him. His long tear-filled silences, his looking up to the heavens: these were so he could read his cue

cards, he would later often say. He didn't know his lines and he had to read them somehow, so they had stuck them to the ceiling for him. Nevertheless, "It is Brando talking about himself, being himself," as Christian Marquand, his best friend, the closest of the close, put it plainly.[132] "I might be able to comprehend the universe, but… I'll never discover the truth about you. Never. I mean, who the hell were you?" Thus begins a monologue that we know from Bertolucci was largely written by Brando himself. A moment all the more amazing for seeming to be a dialogue: the two of them talking past each other, but a dialogue all the same, where a response is expected, where the questions are not rhetorical but seem to take shape in the thick silence. Paul reminds his dead wife how he seduced her—"Remember?"—rants and raves about her horrible desertion—"I hope you rot in hell. […] You know why? Because you lied. You lied to me and I trusted you"—and passes from insult to supplication—"Go on, tell me you didn't lie. Haven't you got anything to say about that? […] Go on, tell me. […] Tell me something sweet. Smile at me and say I just misunderstood…" His voice shifts from harshness to tenderness, from intimate disclosure to abuse, like the instrument of a great artist. During most of the scene, Bertolucci refrains from filming in close-up, using it only at the moment of the real breakdown, when Paul cries and explains, "I'm sorry… I just can't… I can't stand it… to see these goddamn things on

your face," before touching the dead woman's face as he has never done with Jeanne's, with infinite tenderness. "Rosa… Oh, God!" He leans toward her and rests his head on her silent heart. "I'm sorry. I don't know why you did it."

From Nonchalance to Tragedy

After that kind abandonment, such a stunning declaration of love, the false joy that comes before the final tragedy hardly fools us. Like a child once more, Paul delights in shocking the mostly elderly patrons of the tango ballroom where he's dragged Jeanne. He makes his young partner dance, improvising off-the-wall moves. We rediscover the facetious Brando of his younger days; his body suddenly seems lighter, the sadness in his eyes less apparent. When Jeanne announces that she intends to leave him, that she's getting married, Paul is having none of it. He chases her all the way home where, with gum in his mouth, he looks like an adolescent having a good time. We see him proclaim, like the passionate romantic he never succeeded in being, "You ran through Africa and Asia and Indonesia. And now I've found you. And I love you. I wanna know your name." Jeanne whispers her first name as she shoots him fatally with a revolver. Paul steps toward the window mumbling, "Our children… will remember…" He goes out onto the balcony and sticks his gum on the wrought

iron railing. He faces the camera and gives us, us much more than Jeanne, a final look of distress.

Once he got past the exhilaration of making it, the film had a bitter aftertaste for Brando. "I will never make another film like that one," he said. "For the first time, I have felt a violation of my innermost self. It should be the last time."[133] He did return to the spotlight, of course; his work charmed *Playboy* as much as it did the *New York Times*, and the promise of seeing him naked inspired thousands of Spaniards to cross the border to see the film — censored in their country — in Biarritz or Perpignan. Pauline Kael, in her now famous ode to this one-of-a-kind film, paid tribute to him: "When Brando improvises within Bertolucci's structure, his full art is realized. His performance is not like Mailer's acting but like Mailer's best writing: intuitive, rapt, princely. On the screen Brando is our genius as Mailer is our genius in literature."[134] What other actor has ever received such high accolades or seen his work compared to great literature, his performance praised to the skies like that of a major artist? And yet, in the eyes of Brando himself, it was all worth nothing compared to the ordeal represented by his character in this film, the vision of this Paul as a slave to his urges, to his past, to his pain. In the end, there's nothing surprising about this: who wants to see a silhouette of himself broken by life's cruelty, as an aging and suicidal creature, in short, as a figure in a painting of Francis Bacon's?

10

Colonel Walter E. Kurtz

Apocalypse Now (1979)
Francis Ford Coppola

"Horror has a face. And you must make
a friend of horror."
—Colonel Walter E. Kurtz

One fine day in the fall of 1976, during the interminable filming of *Apocalypse Now*, Marlon Brando decided to organize a big party in the villa the producers had rented for him on the coast of Manila. Four hundred guests were invited. The full cast was there, from Martin Sheen, with his gaunt face and wild eyes, to Laurence Fishburne, a fifteen-year-old kid who had lied about his age to land a role, not to mention the beautiful Aurore Clément who would end up getting cut during editing.[135] There was also the band of feisty Italians surrounding the director of photography, Vittorio Storaro, who'd previously worked on *Last Tango in Paris*; Christian Marquand, that French bon vivant, the master of the house's best friend from way back; and the team's chief himself, Francis Ford Coppola, surrounded by his large tribe — wife, children, and assistants of all sorts. Finally, there were a good hundred Ifugao natives, recently recruited to play the followers of the mysterious Colonel Kurtz. The atmosphere was a mixture of seventies hippie fun and the extravagant glamour of faraway Hollywood. Champagne flowed, the buffet spilled over with food, and marijuana was passed around liberally, as were a few stronger drugs like cocaine and Quaaludes. Should anyone get bored, they were immediately entertained by magicians and musicians hired to liven up the event. The final touch, after midnight: a magnificent fireworks display — devised by the special effects team — lighting up the Philippine sky. No one had a minute to himself… to the point that the strangeness of this sumptuous soirée would be overlooked: there was no trace of the illustrious host. Was it a practical joke? Or was it symbolic? Everyone enjoyed the dishes the star had had catered, drank his alcohol, danced to his music, but no one would catch a single glimpse of him. Marlon Brando, the silent puppeteer of the comedy playing out under his roof, would remain unseen until the end. Did Francis Ford Coppola understand the lesson his favorite actor gave him that night? Was he finally reassured, having at first feared a disaster when an obese Brando stepped off the

airplane, knowing next to nothing about the film he'd come to make? By bringing together a crowd of admirers on his compound and still succeeding to escape being seen, Brando had just demonstrated that he completely understood his role and even that he was, to put it plainly, the very embodiment of Colonel Walter E. Kurtz, a creature of darkness hidden from sight, the all-powerful master of each of his loyal followers.

Conrad's Novella

The credits for *Apocalypse Now* make no mention of it, but the film is an adaptation — a fairly faithful one despite the temporal and geographical transposition — of Joseph Conrad's novella *The Heart of Darkness* (1899). In the Belgian Congo, the narrator, Marlow, is assigned to locate Kurtz, an ivory merchant who has disappeared into the jungle. In the film, this mission falls to Willard (Martin Sheen), who in the middle of the Vietnam War is sent to find a colonel the Army has lost track of. Willard, like Marlow, travels upriver to seek out Kurtz in the depths of the jungle and the darkness of the human heart. The film was originally the project of John Milius and George Lucas, but when Coppola picked it up, he took ownership of it with unequaled passion. And he threw himself into it so totally that his wife, Eleanor Coppola, would call the "making of" film about her spouse's great work *Hearts of Darkness: A Filmmaker's Apocalypse*. The Kurtz in the novella is scrawny, ravaged by malaria, with big feverish eyes that eat up his face. Hence the general dismay on August 31, 1976, when a mammoth Brando arrived — weighing at least 285 pounds. Coppola, obsessed with his subject, had asked the actor to study the script before coming. So the director was shocked when Brando asked him what he was going to have to play: "Don't you remember last spring, before you took the part, when you read *Heart of Darkness*, and we talked." To which the star tersely replied, "I lied. I never read it."[136] Not a very encouraging start, admittedly, but one luckily contradicted by the events that followed. For once in the Philippines, Brando became interested in the project. He read Conrad's novella and proclaimed that now he understood.

With his shaved head and heavy body, Marlon Brando plays Colonel Kurtz in Francis Ford Coppola's *Apocalypse Now* (1979).

To create Kurtz's deathly
domain, Dean Tavoularis,
the film's production designer,
used the structure of the
Angkor Wat temples of
Cambodia.

Opposite: Marlon Brando,
Francis Ford Coppola,
and Martin Sheen on the set
of *Apocalypse Now* in 1976.

Yet he didn't stop demanding Coppola engage
in interminable discussions about his character,
again delaying the shoot, which would last a total
of 238 days and wear out almost the entire cast
and crew.

Apocalypse indeed

Coppola himself was going through a deep
personal crisis. "I'm thinking of shooting myself,"
he shouts in *Hearts of Darkness*, before holding
a plastic gun to his temple. On drugs, depressed,
in the middle of an extramarital affair, he was
anxious about the crushing shooting schedule
of this superproduction whose budget overruns
he had promised Paramount to pay for himself.
As he summed it up: "This film is a twenty million
dollar disaster!" For the opening scene, where
Willard is in a trance-like state in his hotel room,
Coppola asked Martin Sheen to get drunk.
When Willard shatters with a punch the mirror
in which he's looking at himself and injures his
hand, it's the actor's real blood we see flowing
and his confusion expressed right before our eyes.
"Francis tried to stop it […] and I said no, let it
go,"[137] Martin Sheen recounts. After all, Willard
was still searching for the killer inside him. The
atmosphere weighed on everyone. Sheen himself,
only thirty-six years old, almost died from a
heart attack. His brother was called in to help
by standing in for him in certain scenes. Dean

Tavoularis, the production designer, recalled the
"nightmare" that *Apocalypse Now* represented.
To create Kurtz's deathly domain, he used the
structure of the Angkor Wat temples of Cambodia
and strew them with corpses, skulls, and human
bones. "I was living in the house of death that I was
making,"[138] he told Coppola's biographer, Gene D.
Phillips. And yet he was speaking metaphorically,
whereas the Ifugao extras actually slept there
during the entire shoot.

Brando passed through this apocalypse without flinching. After all, wasn't chaos his natural
element? Of course, he had financial demands — a
million dollars per week — and his usual tantrums.
Yet considering everybody involved, he seemed to
have been the only one to remain faithful to himself
instead of going body and soul over to the Dark
Side of the Force. Reading the script, Brando was
skeptical about several scenes. A friend of Coppola's,
Dennis Jakob, was dispatched to the set as a
consultant. For him, the character of Kurtz is a
variation on the legendary figure of the Fisher King,
who must be healed each year to ensure that the
harvest will come. The comparison captivated
Brando, who took part in all the discussions and
improvised scenes on demand. "Initially I found
Coppola's reliance on Brando as a writer dubious,"
Jakob told Peter Manso. "But then I understood
that it was necessary for Brando himself to create
the script because Coppola was just floating. Brando
was in terrible shape physically, very overweight,

➡ Marlon Brando According
to Martin Sheen

In 2001, a new version of
Apocalypse Now entitled
Apocalypse Now Redux was
released. At the time, Martin
Sheen did a long interview
with the English daily *The
Guardian*, in which he shared
his memories of the shoot:

"Marlon wasn't difficult at
all. Never. The only problem
we had was the image, his
presence, but he'd just
dismiss it. He treated
everyone the same—Francis,
me, the guys on the crew.
Also, out of all of us, I think
he'd spent the most time in
the third world. So he was
more aware of the fact that
the world's not made up
of first-class service and
over-privileged people.
I was in awe, because for
my generation of actors
there were only two guys,
Marlon and [James] Dean.
And for Dean there was
only one—Marlon."
From an interview by John
Patterson, *The Guardian*,
November 2, 2001.

but his mind was active and alert."[139] After one
of these sessions, Brando shaved his head, an idea
that rescued his appearance: his obesity had
appeared out of place until then; now it became
indispensible. From then on Kurtz, with his
smooth head and round body, had the look of
a Buddha. From this came the wonderful visual
parallel that Coppola created between the Angkor
Wat statues and Kurtz's face. If Brando's instincts
hit the mark, it's because, despite his seemingly
relaxed attitude, he had decided to play the game
and to make Kurtz his own, imposing on him
his bulky body, his misanthropic obsession.
Why then? Two words, doubtless very close to
his own worldview: "The horror… the horror…"
Thus it's to Joseph Conrad's radical pessimism
that we owe this miracle: a role that Marlon
Brando took seriously, for the last time in his life.

Above All a Voice

Before appearing on-screen, Kurtz already
occupies it; he's on everyone's mind. Willard, the
narrator, is obsessed with him as he treks upriver
to an inevitable encounter with the monster.
The Doors chant that this is the end as images
of war haunt Willard, who recalls in a voice-over
that he's received his mission "for [his] sins":
"Weeks away and hundreds of miles up a river
that snaked through the war like a main circuit
cable… Plugged straight into Kurtz. It was no

accident that I got to be the caretaker of Colonel
Walter E. Kurtz's memory, any more than being
back in Saigon was an accident. There is no way
to tell his story without telling my own. And if
his story is really a confession, then so is mine."
The enigmatic, and for now faceless, figure of
Colonel Kurtz hangs over the film, clinging to
Willard like a shadow. Over an unlikely lunch
of shrimp and roast beef, Willard is briefed by
a table of officers. First, they show him a photo-
graph of the young Kurtz in a beret, his face
sculpted by shadows. Then they make him listen
to a recording of Kurtz. His voice echoes in the
room, leaving long silences between the words.
"I watched a snail crawl along the edge of
a straight razor. That's my dream. That's my
nightmare. Crawling, slithering along the edge
of a straight razor. And surviving. […] But
we must kill them. We must incinerate them.
Pig after pig. Cow after cow. Village after village.
Army after army. And they call me an assassin.
What do you call it when the assassins accuse
the assassin? They lie. They lie, and we have to
be merciful with those who lie. Those nabobs.
I hate them. I do hate them."

The construction of Brando's character depends
on this scene. First, because it plays very intelli-
gently off the mythology connected to Brando
himself. The photo of the young Kurtz is actually
a portrait of Major Penderton from *Reflections
in a Golden Eye*. And that voice, that famous

voice, as nasal and inarticulate as you like, can't help but awaken the viewer's memory. From then on, waiting for Kurtz is bound to become waiting for Brando, a surefire way to guarantee the audience's interest throughout the film. All the more reason for Marlon, when told by Coppola to improvise the monologue Willard hears as a recording, to put his heart into it. He starts with a Surrealist image borrowed from a Luis Buñuel film—"a snail [crawling] along the edge of a straight razor"—and ends with a declaration of war against all humanity—"But we must kill them. We must incinerate them." Here we have the character's entire essence. As soon as the voice coming from the tape recorder says the word "assassins," Willard freezes, his knife suspended above his plate. As in the days of *Julius Caesar*, Brando's voice holds real physical power over others. And when Willard finally meets Kurtz, at the end of this slow trek up the Nung River that constitutes a true descent into hell, it is this same surprisingly gentle voice that he'll first hear coming out of the darkness. The use of Brando's voice and his talent for monologues in *Apocalypse Now*, recalls Truman Capote's profile of the actor from years before: "The voice went on, as though speaking to hear itself, an effect Brando's speech often has, for, like many persons who are intensely self-absorbed, he is something of a monologuist—a fact that he recognizes and for which he offers his own explanation. 'People around me never say anything,' he says. 'They just seem to want to hear what I have to say. That's why I do all the talking.'"[140]

This illuminating passage throws new light on the entire film inasmuch as Kurtz and Brando are the same in this regard. If the colonel soliloquizes, it's because his faithful throng awaits but one thing: to hear his sacred words. When Willard arrives at Kurtz's compound, a landscape worthy of Hieronymus Bosch, he immediately receives this advice from Dennis Hopper, in the role of a tripped-out photographer who's joined Kurtz's cult: "Hey, mac... You don't talk to the colonel... well, you listen to him." Later, an armed man leads Willard, whose hands are bound behind his back, to a room plunged in darkness. Willard kneels in profile before a small alcove from which a cough escapes, a sign that Kurtz is above all a voice. A long forward tracking shot then begins, allowing Kurtz's mumbling to emerge from the shadows:
"Where are you from, Willard?"
"I'm from Ohio, sir."
The camera moves forward and then pans. We now distinguish the contours of Kurtz's body, lying on a bed but still engulfed in darkness.
"Were you born there?"
"Yes, sir."
"Whereabouts?"
"Toledo, sir."
It's then that Kurtz sits up, and in the yellowish light we see the back of his bald head. His face, though, remains in total darkness, and he proceeds with his interrogation:
"How far are you from the river?"
"The Ohio River, sir?"
"Uh-huh."
"About two hundred miles."

"I went down that river once when I was a kid. There's a place in the river—I can't remember—must have been a gardenia plantation or a flower plantation at one time. All wild and overgrown now but... For about five miles you'd think that heaven just fell on the earth in the form of gardenias."

Now Kurtz sits with a water basin on his knees. We hear the sound of washing. The yellow light falls on his head and one of his hands. Then the scene quickly shifts: "Have you ever considered any real freedoms? Freedoms in the opinion of others," says Kurtz as he pours water on his neck, "even the opinions of yourself?" With both hands, he strokes and pats his head, as if to emphasize how smooth it is. He then puts his hands on his face: "Did they say why, Willard? Why they want... to terminate my command?"

Demigod or Pagan Idol?

At precisely this moment, Brando and Coppola complete the task they set out to accomplish: to give Kurtz the stature of a deity. This is how Vittorio Storaro explained why Brando always appears in shadow or very low light. "The Marlon Brando character represents the dark side of civilization. He had to appear as something of a pagan idol."[141] That massive body could have been an obstacle to the spiritual vision of the character; it becomes, to the contrary, a tool. Lying down or making his ablutions, Kurtz always looks like a statue. Only the voice remains, a soft, insistent voice. Those words—"terminate my command"—echo to the letter those of the officers who send Willard on his mission in the beginning of the film. Hence the terrifying impact on the soldier, the impression, *how* we don't know, that this superman was present during the scene. Throughout this dialogue, Brando maintains a flat tone and a disturbing tranquillity. His only recurring gesture consists of stroking his head. When Willard informs Kurtz of his superiors' opinion of him—"They told me... that you had gone... totally insane..."—Kurtz stops for a moment and clenches his fist. But he quickly reprises his little trick. Of course, ever since the long-ago era of *A Streetcar Named Desire*, touching his face has been part of Brando's repertoire of gestures. He uses it to show how contemplative Kurtz is: his voice alone makes itself heard; his body alone makes his presence felt. His existence does not depend on others; rather he is a world unto himself, around which orbits a faceless throng. At the end of this exchange, Kurtz asks Willard:
"Are you an assassin?"
"I'm a soldier."

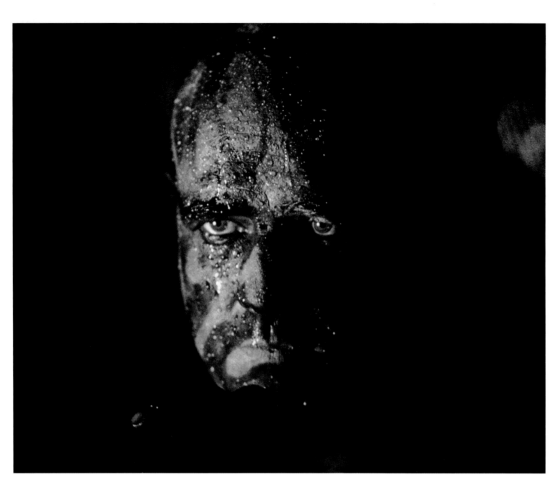

"You're neither. You're an errand boy sent by grocery clerks… to collect the bill."

In the long silence he leaves in the middle of this concluding line, Brando keeps his mouth open. His gaping mouth is a startling image — for it's totally new. Are we to understand that the next word is pending and that Kurtz's voice is inexhaustible?

The critique of capitalist society that crops up in Kurtz's talk recalls the thinking of Brando, who years earlier chose life in Tahiti in hopes of escaping modern society. Coppola plays on this parallel cleverly. We soon find Willard rain-soaked in a bamboo cage, collapsed on the ground, his face splattered with mud, a cord around his neck. A low-angle shot, filmed from his point of view, reveals Kurtz's face completely covered in camouflage makeup. He looks at Willard with perfect neutrality, then raises his chin high, regaining in an instant the look of the Roman tribune in *Julius Caesar*. He closes his eyes, tasting the rain that washes over his face. "A pagan idol," as Vittorio Storaro said, and even more so: a superhuman creature who becomes one with the elements. Suddenly, Kurtz disappears, and the instant Willard opens his eyes again, he discovers on his knees the severed head of Chef (Frederic Forrest), one of the members of his patrol.

Strangely, the obvious monstrosity of the character doesn't discolor our perception of him. Dennis Hopper repeats it again and again:

"He's a great man" that even Willard comes to admire. "He knew more about what I was going to do than I did. If the generals back in Nha Trang could see what I saw, would they still want me to kill him?" he asks himself in a voice-over. And yet what does he see? A talking statue, an oracle who utters enigmatic words, his hand on his head as if to underscore the power of his brain. Kurtz reads as well, seated and seen in profile. His voice comes out of the darkness, skimming over verses of T. S. Eliot:
We are the hollow men
We are the stuffed men
Leaning together
Headpiece filled with straw. Alas!
Our dried voices, when
We whisper together
Are quiet and meaningless
As wind in dry grass
Or rat's feet over broken glass
In our dry cellar
Shape without form, shade without color,
Paralyzed force, gesture without motion […][142]
The editing matches the wonderful slow rhythm of Brando's voice, a voice that listens to itself and that we listen to just as fervently.

The Horror… The Horror…

A second decisive moment then arrives for the character, a confession that reveals how

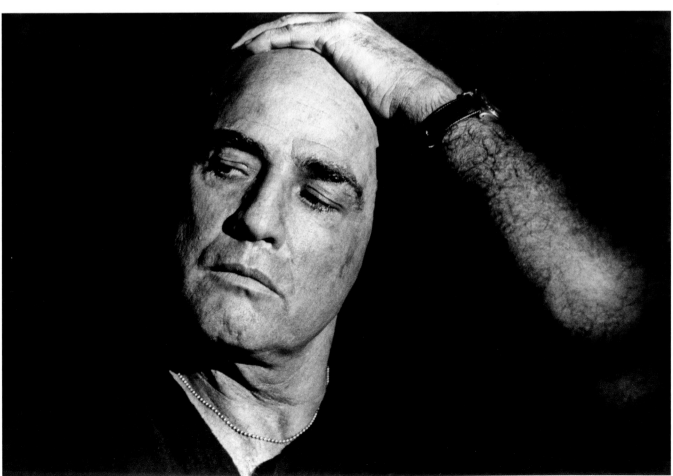

his worldview has changed and the emergence
of his unbridled nihilism. The monologue—
yet another—is filmed in a middle shot, with
a slightly low angle on Kurtz, who is moving
forward. At first we see only his silhouette
shrouded in smoke that makes him look like
a Greek Pythia. Suddenly, he speaks and his
face moves into the light: "It's impossible for
words to describe what is necessary… to those
who do not know what horror means. Horror.
Horror has a face, and you must make a friend
of horror. Horror and moral terror are your
friends. If they are not, then they are enemies to
be feared. They are truly enemies." He recounts
the unthinkable—how, as a member of Special
Forces assigned to vaccinating children for polio,
he returned to the village and discovered a horrific
scene: "We went back there. And they had come
and hacked off every inoculated arm. There
they were in a pile. A pile of… little arms. And
I remember, I… I… I cried, I wept like some…
grandmother. I wanted to tear my teeth out,
I didn't know what I wanted to do. And I want
to remember it, I never want to forget it. I never
want to forget. And then I realized, like I was shot!
Like I was shot with a diamond… a diamond
bullet right through my forehead. And I thought:
My God. The genius of that. The genius! The
will to do that!" During this whole monologue,
a description of appalling cruelty, Brando's
tone stays neutral while his body language is

expressive. He screws up his eyes, suggesting that
the memory is too painful to face. And when he
recalls the mystical revelation that his encounter
with horror represented for him, he places his
index finger on his forehead.

Everything draws to a close during the
native celebrations where a water buffalo is
sacrificed. You'd think you were in the middle
of a deranged version of *Mutiny on the Bounty*,
a nightmarish landscape dominated by the
thirst for blood, where the line between human
and animal has been erased. The ceremony
reaches its climax, but Kurtz remains inside;
his profile stands out like a shadow cast against
a gold backdrop. He records his antimilitarist
maxims, and for the first time his pitch rises,
and he shouts like a man gone mad with rage:
"We train young men to drop fire on people.
But their commanders won't allow them to write
'fuck' on their airplanes because it's obscene!"
Slowly, Kurtz turns his face toward Willard,
who approaches, his own face coated with
makeup. His features are unrecognizable. Kurtz
falls under Willard's blows, slaughtered like the
buffalo outside according to an ancestral rite.
He rears up again, his face bloody. The song
from the beginning of the film comes to mind:
"This is the end," sings Jim Morrison, "[…]
of everything that stands, the end." Kurtz falls
once more. His face, in profile, is finally fully
lit. "The horror… the horror…," he utters,

Dear Marlon,

I got a note from Debbie saying that she brought you the retyped
script and spent a little time with you. I am sorry that I was so
elusive those few weeks I was in California. That time was like a
dream to me, and I was so anxious to get the script done, and solve
all its problems, that I kept putting off sending it and meeting with
you, thinking I would break its back any day. Before I knew it, I
had run out of time, and the whole enormous machinery started up again.
Essentially, what I tried to do, and am still working on was to
rethink the character of Leighley from a doped-up madman, to a sincere,
rational -- maybe even great officer who finds himself totally at
odds with the Generals in command, and gives way to his own instincts
about the way to wage this war. The reason he is in the field, commanding
is by his own choice -- he was called in to settle a Montagnard revolt,
and chooses to 'revolt' with them, to go off, across the border, where
he can follow his own inclinations. He believes the war must be fought
with everything, that it cannot be limited war insofar as the V.C. are
not fighting a limited war. Consequently, he gives way to his irrational
parts, the 'savage' parts in all of us -- sort of like opening a
Pandora's box -- like teaching innocent natives how to kill with modern
weapons, and reawaking almost forgotten lusts for killing and savagery.
But in doing that, he is also kindlxing those near forgotten lusts in
himself as well. Leighley is a extrodinary man, because he always
tells the truth -- but he goes too far, and he is consumed by it. I
guess that's what this movie is really about. About facing the truth,
and then rising beyond it. We will never get past Viet Nam if we
sweep it under the carpet -- we must face it, head on, as ugly and
horryible as it will seem out in the open. And then by facing it,
we can put it behind us. We do not have to feel guilty -- guilt is
a destrcutive emotion -- we have only to judge ourselves, and go on.
And we can't beat ourselves to death about those contradictory parts
of us: the fact that we want things the way we want them, the fact
that we lust after things, and enjoy satisfying those lusts -- even
the lust to kill. The truth is that those things do exist -- but
in balance with instincts of tenderness, compassion, charity -- The
interesting thing about this character is that he is whole he is
irrational and rational all in one, and that is what people are like.

I'm writing this note to you to let you know that I am still working
on this thing, and will continue to work. I have new pages, maybe
they have progressed, maybe not. But, as you know, I have an open
mind and a hunger to make this be good, and to move people, and to
help put this war in perspective. Naturally, I welcome your collaboration
When you come here, I know -- we will relax and take it one step at a
time, and find the way to make the scenes work. The things I have
shot already -- expecially the briefing scene, I think work very well,
and are much more complex than indicated in the script -- I will show
it to you if you think it helpful.
This movie has been a nightmare for me, but I am trying to take it
slowly, one step at a time, letting my inucititions guide me.
I really think you're help at this point, will push me where I xbxxt
want to go. Please don't worry about anything, nothing is impossible,
and together we can accomplish anytinbg, even make a movee about Viet
Nam.
                    Sincerely, FRANCIS

his eyes and mouth open, while Willard—who
seems in this instant to have transformed into
Kurtz—drops his head in his hands.

This Is the End

The glorious execution of Colonel Kurtz is
also the end of Marlon Brando. Of course, the
star—overburdened with money problems—
continued to make movies until his death in 2004.
Pleasant distractions like *Superman* (Richard
Donner, 1978), in which he played Jor-El for
twelve days of shooting and for a record sum
of $3,700,000; those high-water marks of kitsch,
Don Juan DeMarco (Jeremy Leven, 1994) and
The Island of Dr. Moreau (John Frankenheimer,
1996), two films in which he doesn't even pretend
to act; and another, more respectable film, *A Dry
White Season* (Euzhan Palcy, 1989), which he
agreed to do because of its antiapartheid message.
But it is in *Apocalypse Now* that the last flash
of his incandescent genius shines, and that final
gasp—"the horror… the horror…"—sounds
like a philosophical declaration, the conclusion
of a painful private journey, and the ultimate
proof of his exceptional acting ability.

Conclusion

Can we consider an actor to be an author? Regard his assemblage of roles as his oeuvre? This was the question we posed at the beginning of this book. It's a tricky question: as Joseph L. Mankiewicz would say, the piano certainly did not compose the concerto.[143] But it's difficult not to answer yes after following the career of Marlon Brando: seeing him work his way into the script for *A Streetcar Named Desire*, to the point of becoming inseparable from the character of Stanley; watching him transform, so naturally, into a director in *One-Eyed Jacks*; and hearing him improvise the saddest moments in *Last Tango in Paris*. We must also look at the actors who came after him: De Niro, Pacino, Penn, Depp, DiCaprio — so many rare talents who themselves discover the truth of a character somewhere between silence and roaring, lyricism and violence.

In *The Godfather Part II* — which tells the story of the crossing paths of Vito, the father, and Michael, the son — there's a flashback that returns us to the period of the first film, when the Don still reigned supreme over his three sons as he did over the New York Mafia. Here we see the whole family waiting for the old man, to surprise him on his birthday, with all the whispered excitement that surrounds famous people. We hear him coming, and then suddenly he arrives! Yet we get no glimpse of Marlon Brando: Vito's entrance occurs off camera, and the scene ends with the joyous shouts that greet him. Until the last minute, Coppola had hoped the star might agree to dedicate one day to shooting with him. Forget about it: Brando had better things to do on the atoll of Tetiaroa or at his house on Mulholland Drive, and no generosity in store for the filmmaker who brought him back into the spotlight by offering him the spectacular role of the Godfather. With the presence of mind of a truly great filmmaker, Coppola then chose to construct a scene around this absence instead of feeling bad about it. And along the way he offered a brilliant commentary on the star's radiance.

Brando's presence lights up the screen even when he doesn't appear on it. It's a kind of magic we'd be hard-pressed to explain. Everything discussed in these pages — Brando's repertoire of gestures, his acting technique, the emotional depth of his interpretative choices — would be worthless without that intangible and miraculous element that guaranteed, from his first appearance on stage in a supporting role in *Truckline Cafe* to the five minutes he's on screen in *Superman*, that the audience would keep their eyes riveted on him. It's this indefinable grace that explains why, when Woody Allen lists the things that make life worth living in *Manhattan* (1979), he cites only one filmmaker: Marlon Brando.

Following pages:
Marlon Brando around 1950.

1924
April 3: Marlon "Bud" Brando Junior born in Omaha, Nebraska.

1943
Expelled from Shattuck Military Academy, Marlon leaves for New York, where he attends Erwin Piscator's drama school. Stella Adler is one of his teachers.
He takes part in his first shows, performing plays by George Bernard Shaw, Molière, and Shakespeare. Has an affair with Ellen Adler, Stella's daughter.

1946
Appears in Maxwell Anderson's *Truckline Cafe*, directed by Elia Kazan and Harold Clurman, founding members of the Group Theatre (forerunner of the Actors Studio). The play is a critical and commercial failure, but everyone notices the arrival of an exceptional new talent.
Also appears in two other plays: Ben Hecht's *A Flag Is Born* and Cocteau's *The Eagle Has Two Heads*, in which he shares billing with Tallulah Bankhead.

1947
December 3: New York premiere of *A Streetcar Named Desire* at the Ethel Barrymore Theatre. Brando was chosen by the director, Elia Kazan, and the playwright, Tennessee Williams. He shares billing with Jessica Tandy, Karl Malden, and Kim Hunter. It is a hit with audiences and critics alike.

Brando begins six years of therapy with Elia Kazan's analyst, Dr. Mittelman.

1949
On a trip to France, Brando meets Christian Marquand, an actor who becomes one of his closest friends.
Also meets Jay Kanter, who becomes his agent.

1950
Release of Fred Zinnemann's *The Men*, in which Brando plays a handicapped veteran.

1951
Release of the film adaptation of *A Streetcar Named Desire*. During the filming of Elia Kazan's *Viva Zapata!*, Brando meets a Mexican extra, Movita Castaneda, whom he will marry several years later.
Chosen by Joseph L. Mankiewicz for *Julius Caesar*, based on Shakespeare's play.

1953
Laszlo Benedek's *The Wild One*.

1954
Elia Kazan's *On the Waterfront*, for which Brando wins an Oscar for Best Actor.
Death of Marlon's mother, Dorothy "Dodie" Pennebaker Brando.
Brando still lives with Movita but has numerous affairs, notably with Marilyn Monroe and Rita Moreno.
He announces his engagement — which doesn't last — to Frenchwoman Josiane Mariani-Berenger.
Films Henry Koster's *Désirée*.

1955
First (and last) singing role, alongside Frank Sinatra, in Joseph L. Mankiewicz's *Guys and Dolls*.
According to the *Independent Film Journal*'s ratings, Brando is the most profitable star in Hollywood. He receives thousands of letters each year—more than Marilyn Monroe and Clark Gable.
Partners with his father, Marlon Senior, to form Pennebaker, Inc., a film production company.
Meets Anna Kashfi, an English actress raised in Calcutta.

1956
Plays a Japanese man, Sakini, in Daniel Mann's *The Teahouse of the August Moon*.

1957
Joshua Logan's *Sayonara*.
October 11: marries Anna Kashfi.

1958
Edward Dmytryk's *The Young Lions*.
May 11: birth of Christian, the son of Marlon Brando and Anna Kashfi, named after Christian Marquand.
Works with Stanley Kubrick on the project *One-Eyed Jacks*.

1959
Shares billing with Anna Magnani in Sidney Lumet's *The Fugitive Kind*.

1960
Marries Movita Castaneda, with whom he will have two

children, Miko (born in 1961) and Rebecca (born in 1966). While shooting *Mutiny on the Bounty* (1962), Brando falls in love with the atoll of Tetiaroa, which he buys.

1961
Tries his hand at directing for the first and only time with *One-Eyed Jacks*, produced by Pennebaker, Inc.

1962
Divorces Movita and marries Tarita, his costar in *Mutiny on the Bounty*.

1963
George Englund's *The Ugly American*.
Birth of his son Simon Teihotu.
Takes part in the March on Washington for Jobs and Freedom alongside novelist James Baldwin.

1965
Bernhard Wicki's *Morituri*.
Production of Charlie Chaplin's *A Countess from Hong Kong* (1967) suffers from the problematic relationship between Brando and Chaplin.

1966
Arthur Penn's *The Chase*.

1967
John Huston's *Reflections in a Golden Eye*.

1968
Takes part in Christian Marquand's psychedelic movie *Candy*.
Refuses the lead role in Elia Kazan's *The Arrangement*.

1969
Gillo Pontecorvo's *Burn!*

1970
February 20: birth of his
daughter Cheyenne.

1972
Francis Ford Coppola's
The Godfather, for which he
wins his second Best Actor
Oscar (he sends a young
Apache woman in his place
to refuse it).
Bernardo Bertolucci's *Last
Tango in Paris*.
Divorces Tarita.

1976
Arthur Penn's *The Missouri
Breaks*.

1977
Cameo in Richard Donner's
Superman.
Brando makes a record $3.7
million on a two-week shoot.

1979
Francis Ford Coppola's
Apocalypse Now, winner of
the Palme d'Or at the Cannes
Film Festival.

1989
Euzhan Palcy's *A Dry White
Season*, for which Brando
earns an Oscar nomination
for Best Supporting Actor.
Birth of Ninna Brando, the
first of Brando's children
with his housekeeper Maria
Christina Ruiz. They will
later have two more children,
Myles (born in 1992) and
Timothy (born in 1994).

1990
May 16: Dag Drollet, the
fiancé of Cheyenne Brando,
who is expecting her first
child, is killed by Christian
Brando in Marlon's house
on Mulholland Drive.
Charged with manslaughter,
Christian pleads guilty
and is sentenced to five years
in prison.
June 26: Tuki Brando, the son
of Cheyenne and Dag Drollet,
is born in Tahiti. Today he is
a successful model.

1994
Brando's autobiography,
*Songs My Mother Taught
Me*, is published.
Jeremy Leven's *Don Juan
DeMarco*.

1995
April 16: Cheyenne Brando
commits suicide in Tahiti.

1997
Johnny Depp's *The Brave*.

2001
Frank Oz's *The Score*.

2004
July 1: Marlon Brando dies
in Los Angeles. His ashes are
scattered in Tetiaroa.

Page 176:
Top left: Marlon Brando
in 1947.

Top right: Marlon Brando on
the set of *The Men* in 1949.

Bottom left: Marlon Brando
in *Guys and Dolls* (1955).

Bottom right: Marlon Brando
in *The Teahouse of the August
Moon* (1956).

Opposite:
Top left: Marlon Brando
around 1950.

Top right: Marlon Brando
in *Candy* (1968).

Bottom left: Marlon Brando
on the set of *The Nightcomers*
(1971).

Bottom right: Marlon Brando
in *A Dry White Season* (1989).

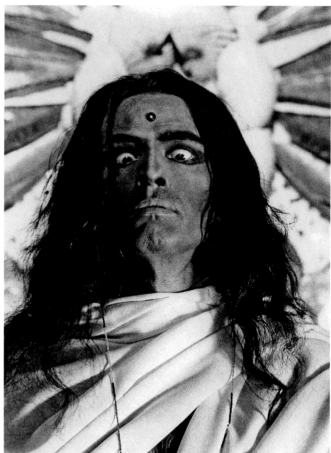

179

COLUMBIA PICTURES Presents
A STANLEY KRAMER PRODUCTION

MARLON BRANDO as
THE WILD ONE ⊗

with MARY MURPHY ROBERT KEITH
and LEE MARVIN
Screenplay by JOHN PAXTON
Directed by LASLO BENEDEK

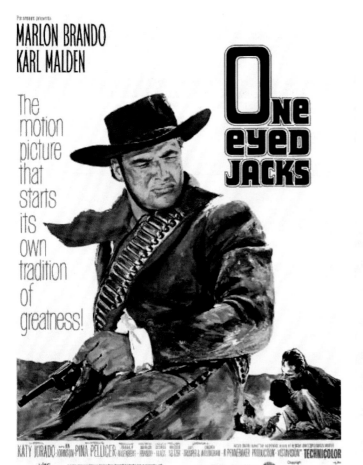

Paramount presents

MARLON BRANDO
KARL MALDEN

The motion picture that starts its own tradition of greatness!

One eyed Jacks

KATY JURADO with PINA PELLICER ... TECHNICOLOR

In the loosest sense he is her husband...
and in the loosest way she is his wife!

ELIZABETH TAYLOR · MARLON BRANDO
IN THE JOHN HUSTON-RAY STARK PRODUCTION

REFLECTIONS IN A GOLDEN EYE

CO-STARRING
BRIAN KEITH · JULIE HARRIS with ROBERT FORSTER · ZORRO DAVID · Directed by JOHN HUSTON · Produced by RAY STARK   SUGGESTED FOR MATURE AUDIENCES
Screenplay by CHAPMAN MORTIMER and GLADYS HILL · Based on the Novel by CARSON McCULLERS TECHNICOLOR® PANAVISION® FROM WARNER BROS.-SEVEN ARTS

1950
The Men
Directed by Fred Zinnemann *Screenplay* Carl Foreman, based on his story *Cinematography* Robert De Grasse *Set Decoration* Edward G. Boyle *Original Music* Dimitri Tiomkin *Film Editing* Harry W. Gerstad *Produced by* Stanley Kramer and George Glass. With Marlon Brando (Kenneth Wilcheck), Teresa Wright (Ellen Wilosek), Everett Sloane (Dr. Brock), Jack Webb (Norm), Richard Erdman (Leo).

1951
A Streetcar Named Desire
Directed by Elia Kazan *Screenplay* Oscar Saul and Tennessee Williams, based on his play *Cinematography* Harry Stradling *Set Decoration* George James Hopkins *Original Music* Alex North *Film Editing* David Weisbart *Produced by* Charles K. Feldman. With Marlon Brando (Stanley Kowalski), Vivien Leigh (Blanche DuBois), Kim Hunter (Stella Kowalski), Karl Malden (Harold "Mitch" Mitchell).

1952
Viva Zapata!
Directed by Elia Kazan *Screenplay* John Steinbeck, based on a novel by Edgcumb Pinchon *Cinematography* Joe MacDonald *Set Decoration* Thomas Little and Claude E. Carpenter *Original Music* Alex North *Film Editing* Barbara McLean *Produced by* Darryl F. Zanuck. With

Marlon Brando (Emiliano Zapata), Jean Peters (Josefa Zapata), Anthony Quinn (Eufemio Zapata), Joseph Wiseman (Fernando Aguirre), Arnold Moss (Don Nacio), Alan Reed (Pancho Villa).

1953
Julius Caesar
Directed by Joseph L. Mankiewicz *Screenplay* Joseph L. Mankiewicz, based on the play by William Shakespeare *Cinematography* Joseph Ruttenberg *Set Decoration* Hugh Hunt and Edwin B. Willis *Original Music* Miklos Rozsa *Film Editing* John Dunning *Produced by* John Houseman. With Marlon Brando (Mark Antony), Louis Calhern (Julius Caesar), Greer Garson (Calpurnia), John Gielgud (Cassius), Deborah Kerr (Portia), James Mason (Brutus), Edmond O'Brien (Casca).

1953
The Wild One
Directed by Laszlo Benedek *Screenplay* John Paxton and Ben Maddow, based on a short story by Frank Rooney *Cinematography* Hal Mohr *Set Decoration* Louis Diage *Original Music* Leith Stevens *Film Editing* Al Clark *Produced by* Stanley Kramer. With Marlon Brando (Johnny Strabler), Mary Murphy (Kathie Bleeker), Robert Keith (Sheriff Harry Bleeker), Lee Marvin (Chino), Jay C. Flippen (Sheriff Stew Singer).

1954
On the Waterfront
Directed by Elia Kazan *Screenplay* Budd Schulberg, based on articles by Malcolm Johnson *Cinematography* Boris Kaufman *Set Decoration* Richard Day *Original Music* Leonard Bernstein *Film Editing* Gene Milford *Produced by* Sam Spiegel. With Marlon Brando (Terry Malloy), Eva Marie Saint (Edie Doyle), Karl Malden (Father Barry), Rod Steiger (Charley Malloy), Lee J. Cobb (Johnny Friendly).

1954
Désirée
Directed by Henry Koster *Screenplay* Daniel Taradash, based on a novel by Annemarie Selinko *Cinematography* Milton R. Krasner *Set Decoration* Walter M. Scott and Paul S. Fox *Original Music* Alex North *Film Editing* William Reynolds *Produced by* Julian Blaustein. With Marlon Brando (Napoleon Bonaparte), Jean Simmons (Désirée Clary), Michael Rennie (Jean-Baptiste Bernadotte), Merle Oberon (Empress Josephine).

1955
Guys and Dolls
Directed by Joseph L. Mankiewicz *Screenplay* Joseph L. Mankiewicz, based on a musical play by Abe Burrows, Jo Swerling and Frank Loesser and a story by Damon Runyon *Cinematography* Harry Stradling *Set Decoration*

Howard Bristol *Original Music* Frank Loesser and Joseph C. Wright *Film Editing* Daniel Mandell *Produced by* Samuel Goldwyn. With Marlon Brando (Sky Masterson), Jean Simmons (Sarah Brown), Frank Sinatra (Nathan Detroit), Vivian Blaine (Miss Adelaide), Robert Keith (Lieutenant Brannigan).

1956
The Teahouse of the August Moon
Directed by Daniel Mann *Screenplay* John Patrick, based on his play and on a book by Vern J. Sneider *Cinematography* John Alton *Set Decoration* Hugh Hunt and Edwin B. Willis *Original Music* Saul Chaplin *Film Editing* Harold F. Kress *Produced by* Jack Cummings. With Marlon Brando (Sakini), Glenn Ford (Captain Fisby), Machiko Kyo (Lotus Blossom), Eddie Albert (Captain McLean), Paul Ford (Colonel Wainwright Purdy III).

1957
Sayonara
Directed by Joshua Logan *Screenplay* Paul Osborn, based on a novel by James A. Michener *Cinematography* Ellsworth Fredericks and H. F. Koenekamp *Set Decoration* Robert Priestley *Original Music* Franz Waxman *Film Editing* Philip W. Anderson and Arthur P. Schmidt *Produced by* William Goetz and Walter Thompson. With Marlon Brando (Major Lloyd Gruver), Patricia Owens

(Eileen Webster), Red Buttons (Joe Kelly), James Garner (Captain Mike Bailey), Martha Scott (Mrs. Webster), Miiko Taka (Hana-ogi).

1958
The Young Lions
Directed by Edward Dmytryk *Screenplay* Edward Anhalt, based on a novel by Irwin Shaw *Cinematography* Joe MacDonald *Set Decoration* Walter M. Scott and Stuart A. Reiss *Original Music* Hugo Friedhofer *Film Editing* Dorothy Spencer *Produced by* Al Lichtman. With Marlon Brando (Lieutenant Christian Diestl), Montgomery Clift (Noah Ackerman), Dean Martin (Michael Whiteacre), Hope Lange (Hope Plowman), Barbara Rush (Margaret Freemantle).

1959
The Fugitive Kind
Directed by Sidney Lumet *Screenplay* Tennessee Williams and Meade Roberts, based on a play by Tennessee Williams *Cinematography* Boris Kaufman *Set Decoration* Gene Callahan *Original Music* Kenyon Hopkins *Film Editing* Carl Lerner *Produced by* Martin Jurow, Richard Shepherd, and George Justin. With Marlon Brando (Valentine Xavier), Anna Magnani (Lady Torrance), Joanne Woodward (Carol Cutrere), Maureen Stapleton (Vee Talbot), Victor Jory (Jabe M. Torrance).

1961
One-Eyed Jacks
Directed by Marlon Brando *Screenplay* Guy Trosper and Calder Willingham, based on a novel by Charles Neider *Cinematography* Charles Lang *Set Decoration* Robert Benton and Sam Comer *Original Music* Hugo Friedhofer *Film Editing* Archie Marshek *Produced by* George Glass, Frank P. Rosenberg, and Walter Seltzer. With Marlon Brando (Rio), Pina Pellicer

(Louisa), Karl Malden (Dad Longworth), Katy Jurado (Maria Longworth).

1962
Mutiny on the Bounty
Directed by Lewis Milestone *Screenplay* Charles Lederer, based on a novel by Charles Nordhoff and James Norman Hall *Cinematography* Robert Surtees *Set Decoration* Henry Grace and Hugh Hunt *Original Music* Bronislau Kaper *Film Editing* John McSweeney Jr. *Produced by* Aaron Rosenberg. With Marlon Brando (Lieutenant Fletcher Christian), Richard Harris (John Mills), Trevor Howard (Captain William Bligh), Tarita (Maimiti).

1963
The Ugly American
Directed by George Englund *Screenplay* Stewart Stern, based on a novel by William J. Lederer and Eugene Burdick *Cinematography* Clifford Stine *Set Decoration* Oliver Emert *Original Music* Frank Skinner *Film Editing* Ted J. Kent *Produced by* George Englund. With Marlon Brando (Ambassador Harrison Carter MacWhite), Eiji Okada (Deong), Sandra Church (Marion MacWhite), Pat Hingle (Homer Atkins), Jocelyn Brando (Emma Atkins), Arthur Hill (Grainger).

1964
Bedtime Story
Directed by Ralph Levy *Screenplay* Stanley Shapiro and Paul Henning *Cinematography* Clifford Stine *Set Decoration* Oliver Emert *Original Music* Hans J. Salter *Film Editing* Milton Carruth *Produced by* Stanley Shapiro and Robert Arthur. With Marlon Brando (Freddy Benson), David Niven (Lawrence Jameson), Shirley Jones (Janet Walker), Dody Goodman (Fanny Eubank), Aram Stephan (Monsieur André).

1965
The Saboteur: Code Name Morituri
Directed by Bernhard Wicki *Screenplay* Daniel Taradash, based on a novel by Werner Jörg Lüddecke *Cinematography* Conrad L. Hall *Set Decoration* Walter M. Scott and Jerry Wunderlich *Original Music* Jerry Goldsmith *Film Editing* Joseph Silver *Produced by* Aaron Rosenberg and Barney Rosenzweig. With Marlon Brando (Robert Crain), Yul Brynner (Captain Rulf Mueller), Janet Margolin (Esther Levy), Trevor Howard (Colonel Statter), Martin Benrath (Herbert Kruse).

1966
The Chase
Directed by Arthur Penn *Screenplay* Lillian Hellman, based on a novel and a play by Horton Foote *Cinematography* Joseph LaShelle *Set Decoration* Frank Tuttle *Original Music* John Barry *Film Editing* Gene Milford *Produced by* Sam Spiegel. With Marlon Brando (Sheriff Calder), Jane Fonda (Anna Reeves), Robert Redford (Charlie "Bubber" Reeves), E. G. Marshall (Val Rogers), Angie Dickinson (Ruby Calder).

1966
The Appaloosa
Directed by Sidney J. Furie *Screenplay* James Bridges and Roland Kibbee, based on a novel by Robert MacLeod *Cinematography* Russell Metty *Set Decoration* Oliver Emert and John McCarthy Jr. *Original Music* Frank Skinner *Film Editing* Ted J. Kent *Produced by* Alan Miller. With Marlon Brando (Matt Fletcher), Anjanette Comer (Trini), John Saxon (Chuy Medina), Emilio Fernandez (Lazaro).

1967
A Countess from Hong Kong
Directed by Charlie Chaplin

Screenplay Charlie Chaplin *Cinematography* Arthur Ibbetson *Set Decoration* Vernon Dixon *Original Music* Charlie Chaplin *Film Editing* Gordon Hales *Produced by* Jerome Epstein and Charlie Chaplin. With Marlon Brando (Ogden Mears), Sophia Loren (Countess Natascha Alexandroff), Sydney Chaplin (Harvey Crothers), Tippi Hedren (Martha), Patrick Cargill (Hudson).

1967
Reflections in a Golden Eye
Directed by John Huston *Screenplay* Chapman Mortimer and Gladys Hill, based on a novel by Carson McCullers *Cinematography* Aldo Tonti *Set Decoration* William Kiernan and Joe Chevalier *Original Music* Toshiro Mayuzumi *Film Editing* Russell Lloyd *Produced by* Ray Stark, John Huston, and C. O. Erickson. With Marlon Brando (Major Weldon Penderton), Elizabeth Taylor (Leonora Penderton), Brian Keith (Lieutenant Colonel Morris Langdon), Julie Harris (Alison Langdon), Zorro David (Anacleto), Robert Forster (Private L. G. Williams).

1968
Candy
Directed by Christian Marquand *Screenplay* Buck Henry, based on a novel by Mason Hoffenberg and Terry Southern *Cinematography* Giuseppe Rotunno *Set Decoration* Robert Nelson *Original Music* Dave Grusin *Film Editing* Giancarlo Cappelli and Frank Santillo *Produced by* Robert Haggiag, Selig J. Seligman, and Peter Zoref. With Marlon Brando (Grindl), Ewa Aulin (Candy Christian), Charles Aznavour (hunchback juggler), Richard Burton (MacPhisto), James Coburn (Dr. A. B. Krankheit), John Huston (Dr. Arnold Dunlap).

1968

The Night of the Following Day

Directed by Hubert Cornfield *Screenplay* Hubert Cornfield and Robert Phippeny, based on a novel by Lionel White *Cinematography* Willy Kurant *Set Decoration* Jean Boulet *Original Music* Stanley Myers *Film Editing* Gordon Pilkington *Produced by* Hubert Cornfield, Jerry Gershwin, Elliott Kastner and Al Lettieri. With Marlon Brando (Bud), Richard Boone (Leer), Rita Moreno (Vi), Pamela Franklin (the girl), Jess Hahn (Wally).

1969

Burn!

Directed by Gillo Pontecorvo *Screenplay* Franco Solinas and Giorgio Arlorio, based on a story by Franco Solinas and Giorgio Arlorio *Cinematography* Marcello Gatti and Giuseppe Ruzzolini *Original Music* Ennio Morricone *Film Editing* Mario Morra *Produced by* Alberto Grimaldi. With Marlon Brando (Sir William Walker), Evaristo Marquez (José Dolores), Norman Hill (Shelton), Renato Salvatori (Teddy Sanchez).

1971

The Nightcomers

Directed by Michael Winner *Screenplay* Michael Hastings, based on characters created by Henry James *Cinematography* Robert Paynter *Original Music* Jerry Fielding *Film Editing* Freddie Wilson and Michael Winner (as Arnold Crust Jr.) *Produced by* Elliott Kastner and Michael Winner. With Marlon Brando (Peter Quint), Stephanie Beacham (Miss Jessel), Thora Hird (Mrs. Grose), Harry Andrews (Master of the House), Verna Harvey (Flora), Christopher Ellis (Miles).

1972

The Godfather

Directed by Francis Ford Coppola *Screenplay* Francis Ford Coppola and Mario Puzo, based on his novel *Cinematography* Gordon Willis *Set Decoration* Philip Smith *Original Music* Nino Rota *Film Editing* William Reynolds and Peter Zinner *Produced by* Albert S. Ruddy, Gray Frederickson, and Robert Evans. With Marlon Brando (Don Vito Corleone), Al Pacino (Michael Corleone), John Cazale (Fredo Corleone), James Caan (Santino "Sonny" Corleone), Robert Duvall (Tom Hagen), Diane Keaton (Kay Adams), Talia Shire (Connie Corleone Rizzi), Richard Conte (Emilio Barzini).

1972

*Last Tango in Paris
(Ultimo tango a Parigi)*

Directed by Bernardo Bertolucci *Screenplay* Bernardo Bertolucci, Franco Arcalli, and Agnès Varda (for the French dialogue) *Cinematography* Vittorio Storaro *Set Decoration* Philippe Turlure *Original Music* Gato Barbieri *Film Editing* Franco Arcalli and Roberto Perpignani *Produced by* Alberto Grimaldi. With Marlon Brando (Paul), Maria Schneider (Jeanne), Jean-Pierre Léaud (Tom), Maria Michi (Rosa's mother), Catherine Allégret (Catherine), Massimo Girotti (Marcel).

1976

The Missouri Breaks

Directed by Arthur Penn *Screenplay* Thomas McGuane and Robert Towne *Cinematography* Michael Butler *Set Decoration* Marvin March *Original Music* John Williams *Film Editing* Jerry Greenberg, Stephen A. Rotter, and Dede Allen *Produced by* Elliott Kastner, Robert M. Sherman and Marion Rosenberg. With Marlon Brando (Robert E. Lee Clayton), Jack Nicholson (Tom Logan), Randy Quaid (Little Tod), Kathleen Lloyd (Jane Braxton).

1978

Superman

Directed by Richard Donner *Screenplay* Mario Puzo, David Newman, Leslie Newman, and Robert Benton, based on a story by Mario Puzo and on characters created by Jerry Siegel and Joe Shuster *Cinematography* Geoffrey Unsworth *Set Decoration* Peter Howitt *Original Music* John Williams *Film Editing* Stuart Baird and Michael Ellis *Produced by* Alexander Salkind, Pierre Spengler, Ilya Salkind, and Charles F. Greenway. With Marlon Brando (Jor-El), Gene Hackman (Lex Luthor), Christopher Reeves (Superman/Clark Kent), Ned Beatty (Otis), Jackie Cooper (Perry White), Glenn Ford (Jonathan Kent), Margot Kidder (Lois Lane).

1979

Apocalypse Now

Directed by Francis Ford Coppola *Screenplay* John Milius and Francis Ford Coppola, based on a novel by Joseph Conrad *Cinematography* Vittorio Storaro *Set Decoration* George R. Nelson *Original Music* Carmine Coppola *Film Editing* Walter Munch, Gerald B. Greenberg, and Lisa Fruchtman *Produced by* Francis Ford Coppola, John Ashley, Fred Roos, Gray Frederickson, and Tom Sternberg. With Marlon Brando (Colonel Walter E. Kurtz), Martin Sheen (Captain Benjamin L. Willard), Robert Duvall (Lieutenant Colonel Bill Kilgore), Frederic Forrest (Jay "Chef" Hicks, Laurence Fishburne (Tyrone "Clean" Miller), Albert Hall (Chief Phillips).

1980

The Formula

Directed by John G. Avildsen *Screenplay* Steve Shagan, based on his novel *Cinematography* James Crabe *Set Decoration* Lee Poll *Original Music* Bill Conti *Film Editing* John Carter, David Bretherton, and John G. Avildsen *Produced by* Steve Shagan and Ken Swor. With Marlon Brando (Adam Steiffel), George C. Scott (Lieutenant Barney Caine), Marthe Keller (Lisa Spangler), John Gielgud (Dr. Abraham Esau).

1989

A Dry White Season

Directed by Euzhan Palcy *Screenplay* Colin Welland and Euzhan Palcy, based on a novel by André Brink *Cinematography* Kelvin Pike and Pierre-William Glenn *Set Decoration* Peter James *Original Music* Dave Grusin *Film Editing* Glenn Cunningham and Sam O'Steen *Produced by* Paula Weinstein, Tim Hampton, and Mary Selway. With Marlon Brando (Ian McKenzie), Donald Sutherland (Ben du Toit), Janet Suzman (Susan du Toit), Zakes Mokae (Stanley Makhaya), Jürgen Prochnow (Captain Stolz), Susan Sarandon (Melanie Bruwer).

1990

The Freshman

Directed by Andrew Bergman *Screenplay* Andrew Bergman *Cinematography* William A. Fraker *Set Decoration* Gordon Sim and Gary J. Brink *Original Music* David Newman *Film Editing* Barry Malkin *Produced by* Mike Lobell. With Marlon Brando (Carmine Sabatini), Matthew Broderick (Clark Kellogg), Bruno Kirby (Victor Ray), Penelope Ann Miller (Tina Sabatini), Maximilian Schell (Larry London/Hans).

1992

*Christopher Colombus:
The Discovery*

Directed by John Glen *Screenplay* John Briley, Cary Bates, and Mario Puzo, based on a story by Mario Puzo *Cinematography* Alec Mills *Original Music* Cliff Eidelman *Film Editing* Matthew Glen *Produced by* Alexander Salkind, Ilya Salkind, Bob Simmonds, Jane Chaplin, and Maria Gatti de Monreal. With Marlon Brando (Tomas de Torquemada), Tom Selleck (King Ferdinand), Georges Corraface (Christopher Colombus), Rachel Ward (Queen Isabella), Robert Davi (Martin Pinzon), Catherine Zeta-Jones (Beatriz).

1994
Don Juan DeMarco
Directed by Jeremy Leven *Screenplay* Jeremy Leven, based on the character of Don Juan by Lord Byron *Cinematography* Ralf D. Bode *Set Decoration* Maggie Martin *Original Music* Michel Kamen and Robert John Lange *Film Editing* Antony Gibbs *Produced by* Francis Ford Coppola, Fred Fuchs, Patrick J. Palmer, Michael De Luca, Robert F. Newmyer, Ruth Vitale, Brian Reilly, and Jeffrey Silver. With Marlon Brando (Dr. Jack Mickler), Johnny Depp (Don Juan), Faye Dunaway (Marilyn Mickler), Géraldine Pailhas (Doña Ana), Bob Dishy (Dr. Paul Showalter).

1996
The Island of Dr. Moreau
Directed by John Frankenheimer *Screenplay* Richard Stanley and Ron Hutchinson, based on a novel by H. G. Wells *Cinematography* William A. Fraker *Set Decoration* Lesley Crawford and Beverley Dunn *Original Music* Gary Chang *Film Editing* Paul Rubell, Adam P. Scott, and Thom Noble *Produced by* Edward R. Pressman, Claire Rudnick Polstein, and Tim Zinnemann. With Marlon Brando (Dr. Moreau), David Thewlis (Edward Douglas), Fairuza Balk (Aissa), Val Kilmer (Montgomery).

1997
The Brave
Directed by Johnny Depp *Screenplay* Paul McCudden, Johnny Depp, and D. P. Depp, based on a novel by Gregory McDonald *Cinematography* Vilko Filac and Eugene D. Shlugleit *Set Decoration* Miljen Kljakovic *Original Music* Iggy Pop *Film Editing* Pasquale Buba and Hervé Schneid *Produced by* Charles Evans Jr., Carroll Kemp, Jeremy Thomas, Diane Batson-Smith, and Buck Holland. With Marlon Brando (McCarthy), Johnny Depp (Raphael), Marshall Bell (Larry), Elpidia Carrillo (Rita), Frederic Forrest (Lou Sr.).

1998
Free Money
Directed by Yves Simoneau *Screenplay* Tony Peck and Joseph Brutsman *Cinematography* David Franco *Original Music* Mark Isham *Film Editing* Yves Langlois *Produced by* Nicolas Clermont, Tony Peck, Joseph Brutsman, Elie Samaha, Shane Stanley, Bret Michaels, Stewart Harding, and Richard Lalonde. With Marlon Brando (Warden Sven "The Swede" Sorenson), Donald Sutherland (Judge Rolf Rausenberg), Charlie Sheen (Bud Dyerson), Thomas Haden Church (Larry), Mira Sorvino (Agent Karen Polarski).

2001
The Score
Directed by Franz Oz *Screenplay* Kario Salem, Lem Dobbs, and Scott Marshall Smith, based on a story by Daniel E. Taylor and Kario Salem *Cinematography* Rob Hahn *Set Decoration* K. C. Fox *Original Music* Howard Shore *Film Editing* Richard Pearson *Produced by* Gary Foster, Lee Rich, Adam Platnick, Bernard Williams, and Roland Pellegrino. With Marlon Brando (Max Baron), Robert De Niro (Nick Wells), Edward Norton (Jack Teller), Angela Bassett (Diane), Gary Farmer (Burt).

Bibliography

Articles

Truman Capote, "The Duke in His Domain," *The New Yorker*, November 9, 1957.

Jonathan Cott, "Elizabeth Taylor: The Lost Interview," *Rolling Stone*, March 29, 2011.

Guy Flatley, "The Day Bertolucci Felt All Tangoed Out," *The New York Times*, February 11, 1973.

Pauline Kael, "Tango," *The New Yorker*, October 28, 1972.

Derek Malcolm, "Bernardo Bertolucci: Last Tango in Paris," *The Guardian*, September 14, 2000.

David Thomson, "The Method in His Madness," *The New York Times*, July 3, 2004.

Books

Stella Adler, Howard Kissel (ed.), *The Art of Acting*, Applause Theatre Book Publishers, 2000.

Peter Bogdanovich, *Who the Hell's in It: Conversations with Hollywood's Legendary Actors*, Ballantine Books, 2005.

Patricia Bosworth, *Montgomery Clift: A Biography*, Limelight Editions, 2004.

Melvyn Bragg, *Rich: The Life of Richard Burton*, Hodder Paperbacks, 1989.

Marlon Brando, *Songs My Mother Taught Me*, Random House, 1994.

Terry Coleman, *Olivier*, Bloomsbury, 2006.

Jonathan Croall, *John Gielgud: Matinee Idol to Movie Star*, Methuen Drama, 2011.

Natasha Fraser-Cavassoni, *Sam Spiegel: The Biography of a Hollywood Legend*, Time Warner Paperbacks, 2004.

Lawrence Grobel, *The Hustons*, C. Scribner's Sons, 1989.

Lawrence Grobel, *Conversations with Brando*, Bloomsbury, 1991.

John Houseman, *Front and Center*, Simon & Schuster, 1979.

John Huston, *An Open Book*, Knopf, 1980.

Sandra R. Joshel, Margaret Malamud, and Donald T. McGuire Jr. (eds.), *Imperial Projections: Ancient Rome in Modern Popular Culture*, The Johns Hopkins University Press, 2001.

James Kaplan, *Frank: The Voice*, Doubleday, 2010.

Elia Kazan, *A Life*, Knopf, 1988.

Carson McCullers, *Reflections in a Golden Eye* (1941), Mariner Books, 2000.

Peter Manso, *Brando: The Biography*, Hyperion Books, 1994.

Pascal Mérigeau, *Mankiewicz*, Denoël, 1993.

Gene D. Phillips, *Godfather: The Intimate Francis Ford Coppola*, The University Press of Kentucky, 2004.

Robert Sellers, *Hellraisers: The Life and Inebriated Times of Richard Burton, Richard Harris, Peter O'Toole, and Oliver Reed*, Preface, 2008.

Stendhal, *Vie de Napoléon (Fragments)*, Éditions Balzac, 1876 (posthumous work).

Alexander Walker, *Vivien: The Life of Vivien Leigh* (1987), Grove Press, 1994.

Thomas Wieder, *Les Sorcières de Hollywood: Chasse aux rouges and listes noires*, Ramsay Poche Cinéma, 2008.

Tennessee Williams, *A Streetcar Named Desire* (1947), Penguin Books, 2000.

Tennessee Williams, *Memoirs* (1975), Penguin Modern Classics, 2007.

Virginia Wright Wexman, *Creating the Couple: Love, Marriage, and Hollywood Performance*, Princeton University Press, 1993.

1 Truman Capote, "The Duke in His Domain," *The New Yorker*, November 9, 1957.

2 Marlon Brando, *Songs My Mother Taught Me*, Random House, 1994.

3 Peter Manso, *Brando: The Biography*, Hyperion Books, 1994, p. 20.

4 *Ibid.*, p. 29.

5 Elia Kazan, *A Life*, Knopf, 1988, p. 143.

6 Peter Bogdanovich, *Who the Hell's in It: Conversations with Hollywood's Legendary Actors*, Ballantine Books, 2005, p. 82.

7 Presentation of the Stella Adler Method on the Web site of her acting school, The Stella Adler Studio of Acting, New York (www.stellaadler.com).

8 Stella Adler, Howard Kissel (ed.), *The Art of Acting*, Applause Theatre Book Publishers, 2000.

9 Elia Kazan, *op. cit.*, p. 538.

10 David Thomson, "The Method in His Madness," *The New York Times*, July 3, 2004.

11 Elia Kazan, *op cit.*, p. 347.

12 *Variety*, December 7, 2009.

13 Peter Bogdanovich, *op. cit.*, p. 84.

14 "O'Neill Status Won by Author of *Streetcar*," *New York Herald Tribune*, December 4, 1947.

15 "Theater," *The New Yorker*, December 13, 1947.

16 Elia Kazan, *op. cit.*, p. 347.

17 A huge success at the Ethel Barrymore Theatre in 1992, which in 1995 led to a television version by Glenn Jordan (Stanley: Alec Baldwin; Blanche: Jessica Lange; Mitch: John Goodman; Stella: Diane Lane).

18 Truman Capote, *op. cit.*

19 Elia Kazan, *op. cit.*, p. 430.

20 *Truckline Cafe* by Maxwell Anderson was directed in 1946 by Harold Clurman in an Elia Kazan production. It was in this show that Marlon Brando and Karl Malden made their debuts, in minor roles.

21 Truman Capote, *op. cit.*

22 Bonus feature of the French DVD *A Streetcar Named Desire*.

23 Tennessee Williams, *Memoirs* (1975), Penguin Modern Classics, 2007, p. 131.

24 Tennessee Williams, *A Streetcar Named Desire* (1947), Penguin Books, 2000, p. 128.

25 Peter Manso, *op. cit.*, p. 252.

26 Elia Kazan, *op. cit.*, p. 345.

27 Peter Manso, *op. cit.*, p. 251.

28 Elia Kazan, *op. cit.*, p. 346.

29 *Ibid.*, p. 350.

30 Lawrence Grobel, *Conversations with Brando*, Bloomsbury, 1991, p. 68.

31 Tennessee Williams, *op. cit.*, p. 235.

32 She played the role in London under the direction of her husband, Lawrence Olivier.

33 Terry Coleman, *Olivier*, Bloomsbury, 2006, p. 236.

34 Alexander Walker, *Vivien: The Life of Vivien Leigh* (1987), Grove Press, 1994, p. 213.

35 Elia Kazan, *op. cit.*, p. 343.

36 Peter Manso, *op. cit.*, p. 367.

37 DVD bonus feature, *A Streetcar Named Desire*.

38 Truman Capote, *op. cit.*

39 Lawrence Grobel, *op. cit.*, p. 68.

40 William Shakespeare, *Julius Caesar*, written in 1599, published for the first time in 1623.

41 Peter Manso, *op. cit.*, p. 323.

42 In fact, Brando was twenty-eight years old when the film was shot in the spring of 1952 (he was born in 1924).

43 Jonathan Croall, *John Gielgud: Matinee Idol to Movie Star*, Methuen Drama, 2011, p. 377.

44 John Houseman, *Front and Center*, Simon & Schuster, 1979, p. 390.

45 Jonathan Croall, *op. cit.*, p. 377.

46 Peter Manso, *op. cit.*, p. 329.

47 Pascal Mérigeau, *Mankiewicz*, Denoël, 1993, p. 178.

48 For eighteen months, from 1934 to 1936.

49 The title of an autobiographical film by Kazan, with Kirk Douglas and Deborah Kerr (1969).

50 About this incident, see Pascal Mérigeau, *op. cit.*, pp. 311–322, and Thomas Wieder, *Les Sorcières de Hollywood: Chasse aux rouges et listes noires*, Ramsay Poche Cinéma, 2008, pp. 98–99.

51 Peter Manso, *op. cit*, p. 328.

52 Pascal Mérigeau, *op. cit.*, p. 180.

53 *The New York Times*, June 5, 1953.

54 Pascal Mérigeau, *op. cit.*, pp. 207–208.

55 Martin M. Winkler, "The Roman Empire in American Cinema after 1945," in Sandra R. Joshel, Margaret Malamud, and Donald T. McGuire Jr. (eds.), *Imperial Projections: Ancient Rome in Modern Popular Culture*, The Johns Hopkins University Press, 2001, p. 58.

56 Peter Manso, *op. cit.*, p. 270.

57 William Shakespeare, *Julius Caesar*, act III, scene 1.

58 See the previous chapter on the film *Julius Caesar* and Mark Antony. Elia Kazan had given eight names during his second summoning before the House Un-American Activities Commission on April 11, 1952. This made him, according to Thomas Wieder, one of the "most laconic informers" of the witch hunt, even if he remains today the most famous and the most detested. Thomas Wieder, *op. cit.*, p. 115.

59 Natasha Fraser-Cavassoni, *Sam Spiegel: The Biography of a

Hollywood Legend, Time Warner Paperback, 2004, p. 166.

60 James Kaplan, *Frank: The Voice*, Doubleday, 2010, p. 647.

61 Natasha Fraser-Cavassoni, *op. cit.*, p. 166.

62 The main character in a best-selling novel, *What Makes Sammy Run?* (1941) by Budd Schulberg, the screenwriter of *On the Waterfront*. Sammy Glick is a Hollywood producer without scruples.

63 James Kaplan, *op. cit.*, pp. 649–650.

64 Thomas Wieder, *op. cit.*, p. 108.

65 Elia Kazan, *op. cit.*, p. 500.

66 Peter Manso, *op. cit.*, p. 362.

67 *Ibid.*, p. 363.

68 *Ibid.*

69 *Ibid.*, p. 366.

70 In contrast to 1973 when Marlon Brando, recognized for his role in *The Godfather*, sent a young Apache, Sacheen Littlefeather, to the Oscar ceremony in his stead. She refused the Oscar and afterward read a long speech written by the actor that explained his refusal by citing "the treatment of American Indians today by the film industry."

71 A French film on the subject preceded the one by Henry Koster: *Le Destin fabuleux de Désirée Clary* (1942) by Sacha Guitry, with Gaby Morlay and Jean-Louis Barrault.

72 Stendhal, *Vie de Napoléon (Fragments)*, Éditions Balzac, 1876 (posthumous work), p. 45.

73 Stendhal, *op. cit.*, p. 1.

74 Peter Manso, *op. cit.*, p. 398.

75 Stendhal, *op. cit.*, p. 26.

76 *Ibid.*

77 Truman Capote, *op. cit.*

78 Pennebaker was the maiden name of his mother, Dodie.

79 Peter Manso, *op. cit.*, p. 475.

80 *Ibid.*, p. 479.

81 *Ibid.*, p. 483.

82 Lawrence Grobel, *op. cit.*, pp. 58–60.

83 Depressive since adolescence, Pina Pellicer (twenty-seven years old at the time of *One-Eyed Jacks*) committed suicide in December 1964.

84 Virginia Wright Wexman, *Creating the Couple: Love, Marriage, and Hollywood Performance*, Princeton University Press, 1993, p. 242.

85 Peter Manso, *op. cit.*, p. 389.

86 Lawrence Grobel, *op. cit.*, p. 63.

87 Truman Capote, *op. cit.*

88 Lawrence Grobel, *op. cit.*, p. 19.

89 *Playboy*, January 1979.

90 Lawrence Grobel, *op. cit.*, p. 11.

91 Peter Manso, *op. cit.*, p. 529.

92 *Ibid.*, p. 518.

93 Robert Sellers, *Hellraisers: The Life and Inebriated Times of Richard Burton, Richard Harris, Peter O'Toole, and Oliver Reed*, Preface, 2008, pp. 78–79.

94 Elia Kazan, *op. cit.*, p. 255.

95 Carson McCullers, *Reflections in a Golden Eye* (1941), Mariner Books, 2000.

96 Patricia Bosworth, *Montgomery Clift: A Biography*, Limelight Editions, 2004, p. 401.

97 *Ibid.*

98 *Ibid.*, p. 263.

99 *Ibid.*, p. 262.

100 Tennessee Williams, *op. cit.*, p. 96.

101 Peter Manso, *op. cit.*, p. 446.

102 Patricia Bosworth, *op. cit.*, p. 320.

103 Peter Manso, *op. cit.*, p. 448.

104 John Huston, *An Open Book*, Knopf, 1980, p. 331.

105 Interview by Jonathan Cott in 1987 and published under the title: "Elizabeth Taylor: The Lost Interview," *Rolling Stone*, March 29, 2011.

106 Peter Manso, *op. cit.*, p. 633.

107 John Huston, *op. cit.*, p. 331.

108 Lawrence Grobel, *The Hustons*, C. Scribner's Sons, 1989, p. 581.

109 Peter Manso, *op. cit.*, p. 633–634.

110 Melvyn Bragg, *Rich: The Life of Richard Burton*, Hodder Paperbacks, 1989, p. 223.

111 Gene D. Phillips, *Godfather: The Intimate Francis Ford Coppola*, The University Press of Kentucky, 2004, p. 94.

112 The spelling can be misleading: Brando is an Alsatian name originally written Brandeau. On his mother's side, Brando was of Irish descent.

113 Gene D. Phillips, *op. cit.*, p. 94.

114 Peter Manso, *op. cit*, p. 711.

115 *Ibid.*, p. 712.

116 *Ibid.*, p. 719.

117 *Ibid.*, p. 716.

118 *Ibid.*, p. 711.

119 *Ibid.*, pp. 712–713.

120 Audio commentary for *The Godfather* by Francis Ford Coppola (DVD).

121 Peter Manso, *op. cit.*, p. 710.

122 Gene D. Phillips, *op. cit.*, p. 99.

123 See the chapter on the film *On the Waterfront* and the character of Terry Malloy.

124 This happens to be the only time in the film where it's obvious that Marlon Brando is much younger than his character: the close-up of his eyes, ordinarily shrouded in shadow by Gordon Willis but here quite visible, doesn't trick us.

125 Derek Malcolm, "Bernardo Bertolucci: Last Tango in Paris," *The Guardian*, September 14, 2000.

126 Peter Manso, *op. cit.*, p. 735.

127 *Ibid.*

128 *Ibid.*, p. 743.

129 Guy Flatley, "The Day Bertolucci Felt All Tangoed Out," *The New York Times*, February 11, 1973.

130 Peter Manso, *op. cit.*, p. 741.

131 Elia Kazan, *op. cit.*, p. 146.

132 Peter Manso, *op. cit.*, p. 745.

133 *Ibid.*, p. 760.

134 Pauline Kael, "Tango," *The New Yorker*, October 28, 1972.

135 The scenes of the French plantation—with Christian Marquand and Aurore Clément—would be restored by Coppola in *Apocalypse Now Redux* (2001).

136 Peter Manso, *op. cit.*, p. 841.

137 In the documentary *Hearts of Darkness*.

138 Gene D. Phillips, *op. cit.*, p. 156.

139 Peter Manso, *op. cit.*, p. 843.

140 Truman Capote, *op. cit.*

141 Gene D. Phillips, *op. cit.*, p. 153.

142 T. S. Eliot, "The Hollow Men," 1925.

143 "It's about time the piano realized it has not written the concerto!" says Lloyd Richards (Hugh Marlowe), the playwright, to Margo (Bette Davis), his star, in *All About Eve* (Joseph L. Mankiewicz, 1950).

Sidebar Notes

a Elia Kazan, *op. cit.*, p. 753.

b Paul A. Woods (ed.), *Quentin Tarantino: The Film Geeks Files*,

Ultrascreen Series,
Plexus, 2005, p. 25.

c See Patricia Bosworth,
op. cit., and Amy
Lawrence, *The Passion
of Montgomery Clift*,
University of California
Press, 2010.

d Harlan Lebo, *The
Godfather Legacy*,
Simon & Schuster, 1997,
p. 130.

e *Ibid.*, p. 221.

f *Ibid.*, p. 238.

Numbers in *italics* refer to illustrations.

Actors Studio 8, 26, 45, 111, 177

Adler, Stella 8, 10, 13, 14, 21, 22, 24, 26, 27, 177, 181, 186, 187

All About Eve 30, 33, 188

Allen, Woody 69, 173

All Quiet on the Western Front 98

Almodóvar, Pedro 116

Anderson, Maxwell 53, 177, 187

Apocalypse Now 11, 149, 157, 158, 160, 164, 170, 178, 183

Apocalypse Now Redux 160, 188

Arletty 13

Arrangement (The) 53, 177

Baby Doll 54

Bacon, Francis 141, 151, 154

Baldwin, Alec 13, 187

Baldwin, James 177

Bankhead, Tallulah 177

Barrault, Jean-Louis 69, 188

Barrymore, John 29

Baxley, Barbara 55

Beacham, Stephanie 145, 183

Bedtime Story 125, 182

Before the Revolution 141

Benedek, Laszlo 177, *180*, 181

Bernstein, Leonard 51, 58, 181

Bertolucci, Bernardo 86, 141, *142*, 144, 149, 151, 154, 178, 183, 186, 188

Billy Budd 98

Blanchett, Cate 13

Bogdanovich, Peter 10, 186, 187

Bosch, Hieronymus 164

Bosworth, Patricia 109, 186, 188, 189

Boyer, Charles 69

Brando, Cheyenne 11, 93, 178, 190

Brando, Christian 11, 104, 178

Brando, Dodie 7, 8, *10*, 144, 177, 188

Brando, Frances 7, 8, 9

Brando, Jocelyn 7, 8, 9, 126, 182

Brando, Marlon
   Fletcher Christian 11, 92–107, 182
   Don Vito Corleone 10, 11, 124–139, 183
   Stanley Kowalski 10, 11, 12, *12*–27, 29, 45, 53, 84, 93, 110, 111, 128, 181
   Colonel Walter E. Kurtz 11, 156–171, 183
   Terry Malloy 44–59, 93, 110, 128, 181, 188
   Mark Antony 28–43, 61, 181, *185*, 187
   Napoleon Bonaparte 60–75, 181
   Major Weldon Penderton 108–123, 151, 161, 182
   Paul 140–155, 183
   Rio 54, 76–91, 93, 103, 119, 151, 182

Brando, Marlon Sr. 7, 8, 86, 177

Brando, Miko 177

Brando, Myles 178

Brando, Ninna 178

Brando, Rebecca 177

Brando, Simon Teihotu 93, 177

Brando, Timothy 178

Brando, Tuki 178

Buñuel, Luis 164

Burn! 125, 178, 183

Burton, Richard 30, 37, 121, 182, 186, 188

Caan, James 126, *139*, 183

Candy 125, 177, 178, *179*, 182

Capote, Truman 7, 14, 24, 77, 78, 79, 80, 89, 164, 186, 187, 188

Castaneda, Movita 177

Cazale, John 126, *139*, 183

Chaplin, Charlie 10, 77, 86, 125, 177, 181, 182, 184

Chase (The) 125, 145, 154, 177, 182

Clément, Aurore 157, 188

Cleopatra 37, 93

Clift, Montgomery 61, 109, *110*, 110, 111, 116, 182, 184, 186, 188, 189

Clurman, Harold 26, 53, 177, 187

Cobb, Lee J. 46, 47, 51, 181

Conformist (The) 141

Conquest 68, 69

Conrad, Joseph 157, 161, 183

Coppola, Eleanor 157

Coppola, Francis Ford 11, 125, 126, 127, 128, 129, 132, 136, 137, 149, 157, 158, 161, 164, 166, *170*, 173, 178, 183, 184, 186, 188

Cornfield, Hubert 125, 183

Countess from Hong Kong (A) 10, 86, 125, 177, 182

David, Zorro 115, 182

Davis, Bette 188

Dean, James 8, 10, 74, *75*, 109, 160, 161

Death of a Salesman 46, 53

DeMille, Cecil B. 33

De Niro, Robert 135, *137*, 137, 173, 184

Depp, Johnny 173, 178, 184

Désirée 11, 61, 62, 68, 71, 77, 98, 109, 142, 177, 181

Destin fabuleux de Désirée Clary (Le) 69, 188, 190

DiCaprio, Leonardo 173

Dmytryk, Edward 110, 111, 177, 182

Don Juan DeMarco 171, 178, 184

Donner, Richard 171, 178, 183

Donoghue, Roger 51

Douglas, Kirk 53, 77, 187

Douglas, Michael 54

Dramatic Workshop 8, 26

Drollet, Dag 11, 178

Dry White Season (A) 171, 178, *179*, 183

Duran, Larry 82

Duvall, Robert 126, 132, 183

East of Eden 53, 89, 109

Edgerton, Joel 13

Eliot, T. S. 166, 188

Englund, George 77, 177, 182

Evans, Robert 126, 183, 184

Fishburne, Laurence 157, 183

Fitzgerald, F. Scott 8

Fontanne, Lynne 110

Ford, John 33

Forrest, Frederic 166, 183, 184

Forster, Robert 115, 182

Frankenheimer, John 171, 184

From Here to Eternity 45, 111, 132

Fugitive Kind (The) 11, 98, 145, 177, 182

Gable, Clark 93, 98, 103, 177

Gance, Abel 69, 69

Garbo, Greta 7, 61

Gassman, Vittorio 13

Gielgud, John 29, *30*, 30, 34, 181, 183, 186, 187

Gilliam, Terry 69

Girotti, Massimo 141, 183

Godfather (The) 10, 11, 68, 125, 126, 128, 129, 135, 136, 137, 178, 183, 186, 188, 189

Godfather Part II (The) 135, 137, 173

Goebbels, Joseph 34

Goodman, John 187

Grobel, Lawrence 7, 93, 94, 119, 186, 187, 188

Group Theatre 26, 54, 177

Guitry, Sacha 69, 88

Guys and Dolls 10, 33, 34, 67, 86, *176*, 177, 181

Harris, Julie 115, 116, 121, 182

Harris, Richard 98, 182, 186, 188

Heart of Darkness (novel) 157

Hearts of Darkness: A Filmmaker's Apocalypse (documentary) 157, 158

Hirshon, Heimata "Charlie" 94

Hitchcock, Alfred 52, 110

Hoffman, Dustin 128

Hopper, Dennis 69, 164, 166

Houseman, John 29, 30, 34, 181, 186, 187

Howard, Trevor 93, 94, 94, 102, 182

Hugo, François-Victor 34, 38

Hunter, Kim 13, 14, 16, 17, 18, 19, 22, 104, 177, 181

Huston, John 109, 110, 111, 111, 115, 116, 119, 121, 121, 144, 145, 160, 177, 182, 186, 188

I Confess 110

Island of Dr. Moreau (The) 171, 184

Jaffe, Stanley 125

Jakob, Dennis 158

James, Henry 145, 183

Jourdan, Louis 61

Julius Caesar 7, 11, 28–43, 46, 62, 125, 141, 164, 166, 177, 181, 185, 187

Jurado, Katy 79, 84, 182

Kael, Pauline 154, 186, 188

Kanter, Jay 177

Kashfi, Anna 177

Kazan, Elia 8, 10, 11, 13, 14, 14, 18, 19, 21, 22, 27, 30, 33, 45, 46, 52, 53, 54, 58, 67, 77, 89, 103, 109, 110, 141, 144, 177, 181, 186, 187, 188

Keaton, Diane 136, 183

Keith, Brian 111, 111, 115, 118, 181, 182

Kerr, Deborah 30, 181, 187

Kill Bill 85

Koster, Henry 61, 62, 71, 77, 98, 177, 181, 188

Kramer, Stanley 181

Kubrick, Stanley 77, 93, 177

Lancaster, Burt 77

Lane, Diane 187

Lang, Charles 82, 84, 89, 182

Lang, Fritz 33

Lange, Jessica 187

Lantz, Robbie 109

Last Tango in Paris 11, 86, 93, 141, 150, 157, 173, 178, 183, 186, 188

Laughton, Charles 89, 93

Léaud, Jean-Pierre 183

Leigh, Vivien 13, 18, 19, 21, 22, 181, 186, 187

LeRoy, Mervyn 33

Leven, Jeremy 171, 178, 184

Levy, Ralph 125, 182

Little Big Man 128

Lloyd, Frank 93

Logan, Joshua 7, 77, 177, 181

Lucas, George 157

Lumet, Sidney 78, 145, 177, 182

Lunt, Alfred 110

McCarthy, Joseph 30, 33, 46, 182

McCullers, Carson 11, 109, 182, 186, 188

Madsen, Michael 85

Magnani, Anna 145, 177, 182

Malden, Karl 13, 14, 16–17, 18, 19, 21, 51, 54, 54, 58, 58, 77, 78, 79, 82, 85, 89, 104, 177, 181, 182, 187

Manhattan 173

Mankiewicz, Joseph L. 29, 30, 33, 34, 37, 38, 67, 93, 109, 110, 141, 173, 177, 181, 185, 186, 187, 188

Mann, Daniel 125, 177, 181

Manso, Peter 7, 18, 51, 82, 116, 128, 158, 186, 187, 188

Mariani-Berenger, Josiane 177

Marlowe, Hugh 188

Marquand, Christian 125, 151, 157, 177, 182, 188

Martin, Dean 111, 182

Martino, Al 132

Mason, James 30, 33, 34, 181

Mastroianni, Marcello 13

Metro-Goldwyn-Mayer 33, 61, 93, 94, 98

Milestone, Lewis 93, 94, 98, 106, 182

Milius, John 157, 183

Miller, Arthur 46, 53

Mitchell, Margaret 21

Mittelman (Dr.) 45, 177

Monroe, Marilyn 52, 62, 119, 177

Montana, Lenny 132

Moravia, Alberto 141

Moreno, Rita 177, 183

Morrison, Jim 169

Moszkowicz, Fernand 144

Mutiny on the Bounty (1935) 93

Mutiny on the Bounty (1962) 11, 82, 93, 98, 104, 106, 177, 182

Neider, Charles 77, 182

Newman, Paul 8, 45, 183

Nightcomers (The) 11, 145, 178, 179, 183

Night of the Following Day (The) 125, 183

Night of the Hunter (The) 89

Nordhoff, Charles 93, 182

Norman Hall, James 93, 182

North, Alex 21, 181

Oberon, Merle 68, 70, 71, 75, 181

Olivier, Laurence (Sir) 13, 29

On the Waterfront 10, 11, 24, 45, 46, 51, 52, 53, 54, 55, 58, 61, 77, 93, 110, 142, 177, 181, 188

One-Eyed Jacks 11, 54, 77, 78, 85, 86, 89, 93, 103, 119, 141, 145, 173, 177, 180, 182, 188

Oz, Frank 178

Pacino, Al 11, 126, 132, 134, 136, 139, 183

Palcy, Euzhan 171, 178, 183

Paramount 46, 89, 125, 165

Paths of Glory 177, 188

Peckinpah, Sam 77

Pellicer, Pina 82, 84, 88, 89, 90–91, 182, 188, 189

Penn, Arthur 125, 128, 145, 177, 178, 182, 183

Penn, Sean 173

Pennebaker, Dorothy (see Dodie Brando)

Phillips, Gene D. 158, 186, 188

Piscator, Erwin 8, 26, 177

Place in the Sun (A) 109, 110

Pontecorvo, Gillo 125, 178, 183

Puzo, Mario 125, 126, 129, 183, 184

Quo Vadis 33

Reed, Carol 94, 98

Reflections in a Golden Eye 11, 93, 109, 111, 115, 116, 119, 125, 141, 144, 145, 161, 177, 180, 182, 186, 188

Rennie, Michael 68, 181

Reservoir Dogs 85

Rhodes, Philip 61, 128

Richardson, Ralph 29

Ruddy, Albert S. 125, 183

Ruiz, Maria Christina 178

Sayonara 7, 77, 142, 177, 181

Saint, Eva Marie 46, 46, 50, 51, 52, 181

Schneider, Maria 140, 141, 142, 143, 144, 146–147, 148, 149, 151, 152–153, 154, 155, 183

Schulberg, Budd 45, 46, 52, 181, 188

Seely, Tim 103

Selinko, Annemarie 181

Shakespeare, William 7, 8, 11, 21, 29, 30, 34, 37, 39, 128, 177, 181, 187

Sheen, Martin 157, 158, 159, 160, 161, 169, 183, 184

Shire, Talia 132, 132, 135, 183

Simmons, Jean 61, 62, 64–65, 66, 68, 71, 72–73, 181

Sinatra, Frank 45, 132, 177, 181

Sirk, Douglas 33

Smith, Dick 128

Spiegel, Sam 45, 58, 181, 182, 186, 187

Splendor in the Grass 89

Stanislavski, Constantin 8, 10, 26

Steiger, Rod 51, 69, 189

Steinbeck, John 109, 181

Stendhal 61, 62, 67, 186, 188

Sternberg, Josef von 33, 183

Stevens, George 109, 110, 181

Storaro, Vittorio 157, 164, 166, 183

Strasberg, Lee 8, 10, 26

Streetcar Named Desire (A) (film) 8, 10, 13, 21, 22, 24, 27, 29, 34, 45, 51, 52, 53, 54, 58, 93, 116, 128, 164, 173, 177, 181, 186, 187

Streetcar Named Desire (A) (play) 177

Streets of San Francisco (The) 54

Suddenly, Last Summer 109, 110

Superman 171, 173, 178, 183

Tandy, Jessica 13, 14, 18, 21, 177

Taradash, Daniel 181, 182

Tarantino, Quentin 85, 188

Tarita 93, 98, 99, 103, 104, 104, 105, 177, 178, 182

Tavoularis, Dean 158, 158

Taylor, Elizabeth 11, 109, 111, 114, 115, 117, 118, 120, 121, 182, 184, 186, 188

Teahouse of the August Moon (The) 10, 125, 142, 176, 177, 178, 181

Third Man (The) 98

Tracy, Spencer 77

Truckline Cafe 14, 53, 54, 173, 177, 187

Turn of the Screw (The) 145

Twentieth Century Fox 61

Visconti, Luchino 13

Viva Zapata! 11, 53, 82, 142, 177, 181

Welles, Orson 29, 77

Wicki, Bernhard 177, 182

Wild Bunch (The) 77

Wild River 110

Williams, Tennessee 11, 13, 14, 18, 19, 21, 22, 27, 53, 54, 109, 110, 177, 181, 182, 186, 187, 188

Willis, Gordon 126, 128, 183, 188

Winner, Michael 145, 183

Wood, Yvonne 84

Wyler, William 33, 93

Young Lions (The) 111, 177, 182

Zinnemann, Fred 110, 177, 181, 184

Original title: *Marlon Brando*
© 2013 Cahiers du cinéma
SARL

Titre original :
Marlon Brando © 2013
Cahiers du cinéma SARL

This Edition published by
Phaidon Press Limited
under licence from Cahiers
du cinéma SARL, 65, rue
Montmartre, 75002 Paris,
France © 2013 Cahiers
du cinéma SARL.

Cette Édition est publiée
par Phaidon Press Limited
avec l'autorisation des
Cahiers du cinéma SARL,
65, rue Montmartre,
75002 Paris, France © 2013
Cahiers du cinéma SARL.

Cahiers du cinéma
65, rue Montmartre
75002 Paris

www.cahiersducinema.com

ISBN 978 0 7148 6663 5

A CIP catalogue record of this
book is available from the
British Library.

Series concept designed
by Thomas Mayfried
Designed by Ron Woods

Translated from the French
by Lucy McNair
and Brandon Hopkins

Printed in China

Photographic credits

Alamy / AF archive: p. 70; Christie's /
Sipa Press: p. 171; Coll. Cahiers
du cinéma: p. 9, 110 (br); Coll. Cahiers
du cinéma / Columbia: p. 47 (b),
48-49, p. 55, 56-57, 58; Coll. Cahiers
du cinéma / D. Rabourdin: p. 39;
Coll. Cahiers du cinéma / MGM: p. 32,
33, 37; Coll. Cahiers du cinéma /
Warner Bros: p. 14, 15, 20 (t), 23 (b),
25; Coll. Cahiers du cinéma / MGM:
p. 102 (t), 104, 106; Coll. Cahiers du
cinéma / Paramount Films / Pennebaker
Productions: p. 87; Coll. Cahiers
du cinéma / Paramount Pictures: cover,
p. 124, 126, 180 (bl); Coll. Cahiers
du cinéma / The Samuel Goldwyn
Company / MGM: p. 176 (br); Coll.
Cahiers du cinéma / United Artists:
p. 150, 154; Coll. Cahiers du cinéma /
Warner Bros Pictures / Seven Arts:
p. 121, 180 (br); Coll. Cahiers du
cinéma / Zoetrope Studios: p. 161, 167
(t, b), 170 (tl, tr, bl, br); Coll. CAT'S /
Paramount Pictures: p. 139; Coll.
CAT'S / Twentieth Century Fox Film
Corporation: p. 72-73; Coll. CAT'S /
Zoetrope Studios: p. 158, 162-163,
168; Coll. CAT'S / Columbia Pictures:
p. 50 (b); Coll. CAT'S / MGM: p. 42;
Coll. CAT'S / Paramount Films /
Pennebaker Productions: p. 83; Coll.
CAT'S / Warner Bros: p. 108, 117,
122-123; Coll. CAT'S / Warner Bros
Pictures: p. 12, 20 (b); Coll.
Cinémathèque française / © 20th
Century Fox Corporation: p. 64-65;
Coll. Cinémathèque française /
©Angelo Novi: p. 142; Coll.
Cinémathèque française / DR: p. 94,
100-101, 102 (b), 112-113, 143 (t),
145, 148 (t, b); Coll. Cinémathèque
française / Pennebaker Productions /
© Paramount Films: p. 85, 86;
Coll. Cinémathèque française / © 20th
Century Fox Corporation: p. 67; Coll.
Cinémathèque française / © Columbia
Pictures: p. 59; Coll. Cinémathèque
française / © Paramount Pictures:
p. 132; Coll. Cinémathèque française /
© The Associated Press: p. 135; Coll.
Cinémathèque française / © Warner
Bros: p. 24; Coll. Cinémathèque
française / Pennebaker Productions /
© Paramount Films: p. 79 (tr); Coll.
Cinémathèque française / DR: p. 23 (t),
28, 40-41, 69 (l), 75, 81, 88 (t); Coll.
Cinémathèque française / MGM–Metro
Goldwyn Mayer: p. 179 (br); Coll.
Cinémathèque française / Paramount
Films / © Pennebaker Productions:
p. 90-91; Coll. Cinémathèque française /
United Artists: p. 159; Coll.
Cinémathèque française / Warner Bros /
© United Artists: p. 19 (t); Coll.
Photo12 / Archives du 7e Art / DR:
p. 46, 54, 79 (b), 82; Collection
Christophel / Charles K. Feldman
Group / Warner Bros Pictures: p. 18;
Collection Christophel / Paramount
Pictures: p. 69 (r); Collection
Christophel / MGM: p. 38, 43, 99,
105, 107; Collection Christophel /
Paramount Films / Pennebaker
Productions: p. 88 (b); Collection
Christophel / Paramount Pictures:
p. 127 (b), 129, 130-131, 133, 138;
Collection Christophel / The Coppola
Company / Paramount Pictures: p. 137;
Collection Christophel / Twentieth
Century Fox Film Corporation: p. 63,
66; Collection Christophel / United
Artists: p. 143 (b), 151, 152-153;
Collection Christophel / Warner Bros
Pictures / Seven Arts: p. 111, 114 (t),
118 (t, b), 120 (t, b); Collection

Christophel / Zoetrope Studios: p. 156,
160, 165, 169; Corbis / © Bettmann:
p. 76, 79 (tl); Corbis / © Condé Nast
Archive: p. 176 (tl); Courtesy of the
Library of Congress, Washington D.C.:
p. 80 (r, l); Getty Images / Time & Life
Pictures / Ed Clark: p. 176 (tr); Getty
Images / Time & Life Pictures / John
Swope: p. 35; Getty Images / Time
& Life Pictures / Alfred Eisenstaedt:
p. 27; Getty Images / Archive Photos:
p. 74; Getty Images / Archive Photos/
Paramount: p. 134; Getty Images /
Columbia Tristar: p. 47 (t); Getty
Images / Hulton Archive: p. 53, 60;
Getty Images / Keystone / Hulton
Archive: p. 140; Getty Images /
Mondadori Portfolio: p. 174-175;
MPTV / Photomasi: p. 9 (br); MPTV /
Photomasi / © John Swope Trust: p. 36,
185; MPTV / Photomasi / Columbia:
p. 10; MPTV / Photomasi / Paramount:
p. 127 (t); The Kobal Collection:
p. 6, 9 (t), 26, 62, 79, 179 (tl); The
Kobal Collection / Columbia: p. 44, 50,
180 (t); The Kobal Collection / MGM:
p. 30, 31, 92, 95, 96-97, 176 (br); The
Kobal Collection / PEA: p. 146-147,
149, 155; The Kobal Collection /
Warner Bros: p. 16-17, 19 (b); The
Kobal Collection / Warner Bros /
SEVEN ARTS: p. 114 (b); The Kobal
Collection / ZOETROPE / UNITED
ARTISTS: p. 166; The Kobal Collection /
Avco Embassy: p. 179 (bl); The Kobal
Collection / Selmur / Dear / Corona:
p. 179 (tr).

All reasonable efforts have been made
to trace the copyright holders of the
photographs used in this book.
We apologize to anyone that we were
unable to reach.

Cover illustration
Marlon Brando in Francis Ford
Coppola's *The Godfather* (1972).